Fly Fishing
NEW HAMPSHIRE'S
SECRET WATERS

STEVE ANGERS

THE
History
PRESS

Published by The History Press
Charleston, SC
www.historypress.com

All photos by Leslie Angers.

First published 2020

Manufactured in the United States

ISBN 9781467141680

Library of Congress Control Number: 2019954420

CONTENTS

ACKNOWLEDGEMENTS

To "the Boys," who are always looking for the next wild trout adventure. To the "Old Timer," who taught me to love brook trout and the environs they inhabit. To my wife and photographer, Leslie, who has chronicled our adventures for this book. And to my grandsons, Mac and Jack, the future of saving the secret waters of New Hampshire.

INTRODUCTION

As the deep darkness settled over the lake and the fog began to rise off the water, the lights in the log cabin were being lit. The Boys had returned from a good evening of fishing on one of their favorite remote trout ponds. It was time for a couple of adult beverages, some spirited team cribbage and planning for tomorrow's adventure.

"That was a helluva trout you caught right before we left," said the Old Timer.

"He couldn't resist that '88' I was stripping just beneath the surface," said Troutman.

"Where do you find these unheard of flies?" asked Pic.

"If a fly worked fifty years ago it will work today," said Troutman. "No one uses the old fly patterns anymore, so they are new to the trout!"

"I keep my fly boxes filled with Muddler Minnows of all sizes and colors," said Goose. "The trout are still suckers for that fly. I just have to get the right size dialed in."

The Boys always found a weekend to take a traditional trip to fly fish for brook trout. It was a bond they had forged in college, and they tried to continue the tradition. As they got more focused on the remote trout ponds, they needed a fourth person to join the trip, and Troutman's dad, the Old Timer, joined them on the annual expedition. The four were bound together by their love of brook trout and wild places. Each year as it got harder and harder to find a place with solitude and beautiful brook

A prize catch.

trout, the Boys would go farther and farther into the woods. This year they had driven eighteen miles into the Great North Woods and carried canoes a quarter of a mile to one of their favorite ponds. The trail into the pond was washed out and steep. This made it difficult for all but the hardiest and most serious of fly fishers to reach the pond.

"They are going to need to sell parking stickers up there," said the Old Timer. "I have not seen that number of boats there. I guess our secret is out!"

"We certainly didn't catch any of those nice 18 inchers this year," Troutman said.

"I had one on, but it took me right into the stumps and broke me off," said Pic.

"You using that Supervisor again?" asked Troutman.

"You betcha," said Pic. "Fly never fails me in that pond. Especially if I can get it deep enough and close enough to that spring."

"You're always dredging those spring holes, Pic," said the Old Timer. "If I can't catch them on a dry, I can't be bothered."

"Well, at least I'm catching fish!" said Pic.

"You lost the big one though," said Goose. He passed around his iPhone with a picture of a beautiful thirteen-inch brookie.

"That's a fine trout in anybody's book," said the Old Timer. Everyone nodded in agreement. The Boys knew they were blessed to be able to pursue these beautiful creatures. They cherished the pursuit and the bond they had formed.

THIS TYPE OF CONVERSATION takes place all over New Hampshire during trout season. It has been repeated hundreds of times—the characters change, but the pursuit of and the joy of fish stays the same. It is the bond that we all share.

With the advent of Google Maps, YouTube, Instagram and Facebook, it is getting harder and harder to find secret waters. The aim of this book is to share some of the best waters that we have fished over the last fifty years. Many of these waters will be new to you. Many are tried and true waters of the longtime fly fishers. Either way, we hope that this book will raise awareness of the brook trout of New Hampshire and develop that deep love we all have for beautiful fishes and wild places.

So, as you read, plan your adventures and tie your flies, please remember that these are the good old days and that a trout, especially a wild trout, is too valuable to be caught only once.

Hike in ponds hold big trout.

PART I

WHAT YOU NEED FOR A SUCCESSFUL OUTING

The lights were shining through the windows of the cabin. It made Troutman smile. He knew the Old Timer was inside and had opened the camp earlier in the day. Returning to camp was a right of renewal for Troutman and his fishing buddies. Another fishing trip was about to unfold.

"'Bout time you got here," said the Old Timer.

"Traffic down south was crazy," said Troutman. "I didn't break free until I left the notches."

Troutman went into the lodge to drop his bags. He unzipped a duffle and took out a shiny new box of flies. Every year, Troutman tied flies for the group. This year was no different. He slid the box of flies across the table to the Old Timer.

The Old Timer opened the box. He had bought a fly-tying kit for Troutman for his twelfth birthday. He had not bought a fly since.

"What crazy patterns did you come up with this year?" asked the Old Timer.

"I think you will like some of them," said Troutman. "I was lucky to find a jungle cock neck this winter and tied some old-school Hornbergs. Tied them in different colors too!"

"Better be some yellow ones in that box," said the Old Timer.

"Oh, I tied you plenty," said Troutman. "You seem to lose your fair share each year!"

As they looked through the box, one side was completely Hornbergs: original, yellow, orange, wood duck, pink and olive. Troutman remembered how this one fly fished better with jungle cock cheeks. The fly box looked like a rainbow. On the other side of the box was an assortment of old-school wet flies and streamers.

"I dug out Surette's old book and picked out some north country classics," said Troutman.

"Dick Surette taught you a lot," said the Old Timer. "He was a treasure chest of knowledge."

Troutman nodded in acknowledgement. He often went to Surette's Trout and Salmon Fly Index and picked out flies that were as good today as they were when Surette first promoted them in the early 1970s. The Harris Special, Maynard's Marvel, Yellow Dun, Olive Heron— the other side of the fly box was filled with these and other classics.

"We should be all set for another memorable fishing trip," said the Old Timer.

THE FLIES

As the previous conversation shows, there are many ways to approach fly fishing New Hampshire's secret waters. Some of the enjoyment stems from deciding which flies will draw the attention of the trout. There are the go-to patterns, the new kids on the block, the tried and true and the classics. Whichever way you choose to fish, the flies are a big part of the enjoyment.

Big flies mean big fish.

We will share some of our favorite patterns from each category. There are dry flies, wet flies, emergers, nymphs and streamers. Patterns are for the spring (SP), summer (SU) or fall (F). Most patterns have formulas available online. We have added any patterns we suggest that have formulas that can't be easily found to an appendix in the back of the book.

The go-to patterns are the flies that we choose first when we are exploring new water or are visiting a water for the first time in an extended period of time. These flies will almost always illicit a response from fish and give you an idea of the color or size that the fish are finding appealing at the time.

Adams (SP, SU, F)
Light Cahill (SU)
Hendrickson (SP, SU)
Purple Parachute Adams (SP, SU, F)
Griffith Gnat (SU, F)
Black Ant (SP, SU, F)
March Brown (SP, SU)
Trout Fin (SP, SU, F)
Cahill Wet (SP, SU)
Gray Hackle (SP, SU, F)
Hendrickson Wet (SP, SU)
Hare's Ear Wet (SP, SU, F)
Compara-Emerger (SU, SP, F)
Poly-Wing Emerger (SP, SU, F)
Sparkle Pupa (SP, SU, F)

Winged Biot Emerger (SU, F)
Stillborn Midge (SU, F)
Hex Emerger (SU)
Pheasant Tail Nymph (SP, SU, F)
Gray Squirrel Nymph (SP, SU, F)
Fullback Nymph (SP, SU, F)
BeadHead Hare's Ear (SP, SU, F)
Zug Bug Nymph (SP, SU, F)
Tellico Nymph (SP, SU, F)
Little Brook Trout (SP, SU, F)
Light Edson Tiger (SP, SU, F)
Warden's Worry (SP, SU, F)
Soft Hackle Streamer (SP, SU, F)
Mickey Finn (SP, F)
Black Ghost (SP, F)

The new kids on the block are flies that have come into existence in the last thirty years. They are tied with new materials like beads, craft fur and krystal flash. These flies have added excitement to fly assortments and robust discussions as to whether they are even flies at all. We have fished these flies and find them effective in New Hampshire's secret waters.

Brown Klinkhammer (SP, SU)
Olive Klinkhammer (SP, SU)
Moodah Poodah (SU)
PMX Royal (SU, F)
Sedgehammer Caddis (SU, F)
Balloon Caddis (SP, SU, F)

Black Traffic Light (SP, SU, F)
Holographic Red (SP, SU, F)
Spider Caddis (SP, SU, F)
Sparkle Soft Hackle (SP, SU, F)
CJ Controller (SP, SU, F)
Catchall Spider (SP, SU, F)

A wild brook trout fly assortment.

Emerger Caddis CDC (SP, SU, F)
Low Hanging Fruit (SP, SU, F)
Bi Focal Emerger (SU, F)
Spotlight Emerger (SP, SU, F)
Extreme Emerger (SU, F)
Fripple (SP, SU, F)
Rainbow Warrier (SP, SU, F)
WD-40 (SP, SU, F)
Wire Wonder (SU, F)

White Lightening (SP, F)
Phlamin Pheasant (SP, SU, F)
Mylar Prince (SP, SU, F)
Complex Twist Bugger (SP, F)
Rubber Bugger (SP, SU, F)
Franke Shiner (SP, F)
Senyo Trout Parr (SP, SU, F)
Rubber Leg Bugger (SP, SU, F)
Fish Skull Bugger (SP, F)

The tried and true patterns are those that have withstood the test of time. These are the patterns that we are most likely to tie to our tippet when we want to catch a trout. Some of these flies have been around for one hundred years, and some are new to the scene. All of these patterns should be represented in your fly box and will work at any time of the year.

Black Woolly Bugger
Olive Woolly Bugger
Black Wooly Worm
Yellow Wooly Worm

Renegade
Royal Wulff
White Wulff
Dun Variant

Devil Bug
Original Hornberg
Yellow Hornberg
Flashback Hare's Ear
Copper Nymph
Harris Special
Golden Demon
Leisenring Gray Hackle

Casual Dress
88
Leisenring's Tup
Brown Hackle
Royal Coachman
Black Nose Dace
Black Ghost
Muddler Minnow

Finally, the classics. These flies are from decades ago and are patterns that most have forgotten about. We love to fish with them because they are as beautiful as the trout we pursue. We tie these flies, as they are the best reminder we have during long winters that nature's beauty abounds and that the fish they attract are Mother Nature's jewels. Most of these flies are not available at your local fly shop. Try tying them yourself or find a fly shop that does custom tying.

Beaverkill (SP, SU)
Bivisible (SP, SU, F)
Gordon (SP, SU, F)

Little Marryat (SP, SU)
Olive Badger (SU, F)
Pink Lady (SP, SU, F)

A nice assortment of trout flies.

Pink Lady Bivisible (SP, SU, F)

Parmachenee Belle (SP, F)

Wickham's Fancy (SP, SU, F)

Queen of Waters (SP, SU)

Silver Prince (SP, SU, F)

Silver Doctor (SP, SU, F)

Bread Crust (SP, SU, F)

White Miller (SP, SU, F)

Campbell's Fancy (SP, SU, F)

Willow (SP, SU, F)

Greenwell's Glory (SP, SU)

Mickey Finn (SP, F)

Montreal (SP, F)

Gray Ghost (SP, F)

Orange Fish Hawk (SU, F)

Shang Special (SP, F)

Professor (SP, SU, F)

Ballou Special (SP, F)

Whenever we can, we tie our flies on barbless hooks. This makes it easier to release fish and causes less hooking damage. It also saves us from wondering whether or not a water has special regulations. It is always better to be safe than sorry. If you can't find a reliable source for barbless hooks, consider pinching down the barbs of your flies.

We use a multitude of fly boxes. We enjoy the old-school aluminum boxes from Perrine. As those boxes become harder to come by, we have found that the new waterproof fly boxes are effective. We use any size from the smallest day-trip size all the way up to the large streamer boxes. These boxes float, so you can retrieve them should you drop them in the water. Don't forget to open them up after a day of fishing to prevent your hooks from rusting.

GOOSE WAS THE NEXT through the cabin door. He had his one duffle and a rod tube no one had seen before. He went into the lodge room to drop the duffle and claim a bed near the wood stove. He came back to the table where Troutman and the Old Timer sat. He laid the rod tube on the table.

"New rod?" asked Troutman.

"Yup," said Goose with a broad smile on his face.

"What did you get?" quizzed the Old Timer.

"Oh, nothing like that nice Orvis Far and Fine you have," shot back Goose. "I have a beer drinker's pocket book."

Goose took the rod out of the tube. It was a nine-foot, five-weight, four-piece fly rod from Cortland. He assembled the rod and handed it to Troutman. Troutman gave it the wiggle test.

"Not bad," said Troutman. "Nice slow action. That should make you slow down your casting stroke a little."

"I thought I should finally get a graphite rod and join the rest of you," said Goose. "It was time."

Some necessary equipment.

Goose was replacing an old fiberglass rod that was as stiff as a broom stick. He always labored when he cast, and it was tiring for him. He hoped that the graphite rod would be just the ticket.

"I've always enjoyed slow rods," said the Old Timer. He picked up the rod and gave it a shake. He gave Goose his nod of approval.

Rods, Reels and Lines

There are so many rod choices these days that it boggles the mind: fast action, medium fast, medium or slow; mid flex or tip flex; six-foot or ten-foot; one-weight or eight-weight. It's enough to make someone cry. On top of all the actions, you need to find a line that will optimize your rod's power and your casting stroke. It takes a little bit of time to find the combination to match your style, the waters that you wish to fish and the type of flies you want to fish.

Far and away, the number one choice for all-around trout fishing in New Hampshire is the nine-foot, five-weight, four-piece rod. Every major rod manufacturer makes one, and each has its own features and benefits. You need to test cast a rod before you buy it. Most fly shops will let you test cast the rods that they carry.

The fly shop will also know what lines cast best with which rods. This will save you time and frustration. Let the professionals help you make the choice.

Should you get an outfit that just doesn't cast the way you expect, go to the fly shop. They will be able to tell almost immediately how to help you get the most out of the rod and make any adjustments.

During your lifetime of fly fishing, you will own many rods. Some people own more than others. There is a rule of thumb when you get ready to buy a second rod—the 3-5-7 or the 2-4-6 rule. If you started out with the nine-foot, five-weight rod, your next choice for small streams and small flies should be the three-weight rod. Most popular three-weight rods are seven feet. These rods are great for small streams and beaver ponds where trout are small and casting room is tight. The third rod you will get is a seven-weight rod. Popular lengths are nine or ten feet. This rod will handle large flies and windy conditions on large rivers and lakes.

If you are an experienced fly fisher, you may choose to go two-weight rod, four-weight rod and six-weight rod. Lighter weight rods can be more of an advantage with finicky trout but are more of a challenge for casting. There are also anglers who just have one of each weight—two through seven. If fly fishing is your passion, why not?

Just as there are truly no bad fly rods these days, there are no bad reels. The key is to purchase a reel that has a solid construction and is built to last. A good reel will last a lifetime. We have learned the hard way, so we shy away from composite or cast aluminum reels. While these reels are economical, they tend to break easily, and the internals are not engineered to withstand years of use.

Most of the fishing in New Hampshire's secret waters will not need expensive reels with sophisticated drag systems. For all practical purposes, the reel is your line holder. Should you be lucky enough to hook a large fish, you want to have confidence that the reel will not fail.

Most reels today are either mid arbor or large arbor. There are still click and pawl reels being made but they are few and far between. The main thing to keep in mind when buying a reel is to purchase spare spools because you will need multiple lines to cover all the types of fishing in New Hampshire's secret waters.

When you purchase your fly reel, purchase two additional spools. You will need three types of lines to effectively fish all of the seasons. In the early season, you will start with a sinking line. Fish travel the bottoms of rivers and ponds seeking out food before the waters warm up enough to start the bug life. There are various sink rates for sinking fly lines. We choose the three to

Trout hide under big boulders.

four inches per second lines as a compromise sinking line. Faster sinking fly lines are harder to manage in shallower ponds (less than fourteen feet deep), and slow sinking lines can waste valuable fishing time waiting for them to deliver the fly to the appropriate level in the water column.

We are big fans of the countdown method of fishing with sinking lines. Once we throw the line, we will start with one thousand one, one thousand two, one thousand three, one thousand four, one thousand five. We will strip in the fly and cast around the clock from our casting position. If no fish hit our fly, we go up to one thousand ten. Fish around the clock. Then count to one thousand fifteen and so on until we start to find fish. This technique is especially important when fishing the secret, still waters. If fish are feeding the day you are there, you will locate them and catch them.

The next spool for your reel should have a sink tip line. Sink tip lines are designed to help sink flies into the water column. The sink tips come in various lengths, and we like ten-foot sink tips. We follow the same process in still waters as we do with sinking lines, using the countdown method. Sink tip lines are useful in ponds and beaver flowages where depth may be less than ten feet. Full sink lines tend to get hung up on the bottom in these shallower waters.

For moving waters, the sink tip allows you to fish the deep pools or access the water column in riffles and get your fly where the trout are feeding. We find this especially handy for the high waters of spring fishing or when the trout have moved into deep pools. Sink tip lines are great for fishing nymphs, wet flies and streamers. We never go out on the water without one in our pack.

The final line to put on spool number three is your floating line. This is for fishing all those great hatches that we have here in New Hampshire. The line is also great for fishing emerger patterns just below the surface of the water. Dry fly fishing is the most visual and thus most appealing style of fly fishing. Matching the hatch and throwing dry flies has no equal in the fly fishing world.

We try to plan fishing trips into certain secret waters based on the insect hatches. These trips are most memorable. When you can catch twenty-four fish on twenty-five casts of your dry fly, you will never forget the experience.

There are two anticipated hatches in New Hampshire that fly fishers wait for with great anticipation: the hexagenia hatch and the alder fly hatch. These are the final two hatches that give the angler a chance to land a large trout before they "disappear" for the summer.

The Hexagenia is the largest mayfly that hatches in New Hampshire. It is a creature of mud bottom ponds and rivers. These bugs are very large, averaging one- and one-half inches, and are trout candy. These bugs hatch from the end of June into the middle of July. Large still water trout seek these bugs out, and once you have seen a three-pound brook trout inhale your imitation, you will be talking about it for the remainder of your life.

The alder fly, technically a *Zebra caddis*, is one of the few "blizzard" hatches that happen in New Hampshire. When these bugs hatch, they form clouds of bugs over the water. Catching the evening alder fly hatch is another event one will not soon forget. The other great thing about the alder fly hatch is the morning spinner fall. We shake the alders along the river in the morning to have spent *Zebra caddis* fall on the water and get fish rising.

Dry fly fishing on New Hampshire's secret waters is challenging and exciting. We have outlined the hatches for you. Actual times vary due to weather conditions, so use the chart as a guide. Or contact your local fly shop for the most up-to-date information.

Hatch	Start Date	End Date
Early Black Stones	End February	End March
Black Quills	Mid-May	End May
Quill Gordon	Mid-May	End May
Red Quill	Mid-May	Mid-June
Hendrickson	End May	Mid-June
March Brown	End May	Mid-June
Zebra Caddis	Mid-June	End June
Mirus	Mid-June	End June
Light Cahill	Mid-June	End July
Hexagenia	End June	Mid-July
Yellow Sally	Mid-June	Mid-July
Caddis	Mid-June	September
Stonefly	End June	Early August
Ants	August	October
Grasshoppers	August	September
Blue Wing Olive	July	September

Three spools. Three lines. Don't leave home without them!

A word about leaders and tippet. Manufacturers have made this very complicated and confusing. Let's make it simple. Nylon is the standard for all applications. If you want to keep it simple, just use nylon. Use fluorocarbon leaders and tippet for nymphs, soft hackles and streamers—any application where you need to be subsurface and want to minimize line glare.

The White Mountains keep waters cool year-round.

Size tippet can best be determined by taking the hook size of your fly and dividing by three. A size twelve hook uses 4x tippet. A size sixteen hook uses a 5x tippet. The time to vary from this formula is when you know that you are pursuing larger trout and need added strength.

THE BOYS WERE READY to hit the sack. Sleeping bags were rolled out. Beer bottles were washed out and put back in the case where they had started. The fourth member of the group still had not arrived at camp.

"Where is Pic?" asked Troutman.

"Oh, he will roll in at zero dark thirty," said the Old Timer.

"Probably hit a deer driving over this late," said Goose.

Just as the last light was about to be turned out, a loud rattling banged up the drive to the camp. It was Pic. There was something wrong with his vehicle. Goose and Troutman went outside to see what the commotion was all about.

"You called that one," said Troutman to Goose.

"Wow," said Goose.

Pic had in fact hit a deer speeding through Dixville Notch. Fortunately, it was a glancing blow—only lost a headlight. Deer hide was still in the grill.

"Got a late start," said Pic. "I was trying to make up time."

Troutman undid the canoe ropes so he could raise the hood and see if there was any internal damage. They needed Pic's vehicle and canoe to fish the next day.

"She should make it to Shehan tomorrow," said Troutman. "Let's get you inside, get you a beer, and get to bed."

The next day, the Boys packed up and headed to Shehan Flowage. Pic had his trusty Old Town Voyager and Troutman had his Great Canadian. The Old Town was heavy, about ninety-five pounds. Pic had purchased transport wheels to make getting into Shehan Flowage a bit easier. Troutman's Great Canadian was only sixty pounds. He would carry it into the pond.

WATER CRAFT

Anyone who is serious about large trout needs to learn about the still waters of New Hampshire. The still waters are the best opportunity to catch truly large trout. To access these still waters you will need a craft. Canoes can fill the bill, especially if you are fishing in teams. Another choice is the float tube. A newer choice is the one or the two man raft. We like all three.

Float tubes are great for hike in ponds.

Canoes have been the wilderness choice of craft since the first Native Americans figured out how to dig out logs. Dugout canoes were a sturdy craft but were often heavy and not easy to transport. When someone figured out how to peel and glue birch bark to a frame, the canoe game changed. There has been a constant evolution between durability and portability in the canoe game. Only you can make the choice that works for you.

Since the earliest of our fishing trips, a new craft has come to the market: the float tube. Float tubes are nylon-covered truck tire tubes with a yoke to sit in and float around still water. They are light and very portable. They backpack in easily, and if you wish, you can pack them deflated and blow them up on site. They are very reliable and a great choice for remote secret waters.

The newest innovation is in raft-style float tubes. These float tubes allow for better traveling in the water and keep you out of the water while you are fishing. This keeps you warmer and fishing longer in the spring and the fall. They are very lightweight and can also be inflated on site. If you have a hike-in trip longer than a mile, the raft-style float tube is the way to go. Another advantage to the raft-style float tube is that it will carry you to some of the deep holes in rivers that have holdover trout.

We would not have been able to survey the multitude of secret still waters without some type of portable craft. Add one to your arsenal. It may be your most important accessory.

THE TRIP INTO SHEHAN Flowage was productive. The boys dredged the deep holes and drop offs and raised some nice trout. When the caddis hatch started near sunset, the pond looked like it was raining there were so many fish rising. It was one of those nights where there was almost a fish a cast. The boys had Shehan Flowage to themselves, and only the moose knew that they were on the pond. Even with the hike out to the cars, they stayed until they could no longer see to tie on a new fly. It had been epic.

"I lost so many Muddlers on the bottom of the pond tonight," said Goose.

"Same with the Supervisors," said Pic.

"That's the price we pay to catch some of those holdovers," said the Old Timer. "Good thing Troutman had plenty of Hornbergs."

Troutman just smiled. Losing flies was part of the game. That is why Troutman spent the winter tying so many. If you weren't losing flies, you weren't catching fish. Shehan Flowage was an old log pond that held saw logs until they could be floated down to the Androscoggin in the spring. The bottom was littered with old sunken trees—perfect trout habitat.

LOCATING FISH

If you are new to trout fishing, whether it be moving or still water, reading the water is an important time-saving skill. It has taken many years for us to learn the habitats that trout prefer. If you follow these general rules, then you will be into trout sooner rather than later.

When fishing in ponds, the first action we take is to visit the New Hampshire Fish and Game website. A majority of the ponds in New Hampshire have bathymetry maps. These maps will show you the depths of the ponds and where the drop-offs are located. Trout cruise the drop-offs because it is the easiest way for them to escape to the depths after feeding in the shallows. Drop-offs are also the most likely spots to have spring seeps with cold water available year round. Cold water is another key ingredient to finding trout in ponds.

Look at the bathymetry map for Province Pond in Chatham, one of our secret waters. You will notice there is an inlet stream on the north shore where the pond drops to thirteen feet deep very quickly. This is the most productive location in the pond. There are several spring seeps that leach out of that drop-off. We catch trout there all season.

Some of our secret water ponds are crystal clear. You can see down twenty to thirty feet. When your pond is this clear, look for boulders or groups of boulders. Trout like the boulders for cover, and baitfish like the boulders for feeding—it is a perfect combination. Look for fallen trees in the water. Most fallen trees haven't sunk into the bottom of the pond. This provides cover for the trout and gives the trout a perfect hiding spot to ambush unsuspecting prey.

If a pond is new to you and you have brought in a water craft, trolling a fly can also help you locate fish. Trolling lets you cover more area and get a feel for where the trout may be located. We always do a little trolling until we get a pond dialed in. Unlike in Maine, trolling flies is allowed in fly fishing–only ponds in New Hampshire. Don't be afraid to use that tactic.

Reading rivers is slightly different than reading ponds. The similarities lie in looking for quick drops in elevation and looking for spring seeps. Quick drops in elevation usually mean rapids or waterfalls that almost always end in big deep pools that hold trout. Spring seeps also flow into rivers where there are rock outcroppings. Trout can't resist cold, clear water.

Another similarity is wood. Anywhere you see trees that have fallen into the river, there will be fish. Cast your fly as close to the log as you dare and hold on! The strike of the fish will be devastating. We can't tell you how many trout we have caught from under logs in a stream. We have also lost a lot of flies doing so!

The challenge with streams is the variety of habitat and the variability of the currents. Within a mile of a stream, you will see waterfalls, tree falls, riffle water, holding pools, pocket water and seams. Each of these water types hold specific challenges. While most anglers focus on the base of waterfalls, we like to focus at the top of waterfalls and beyond. Waterfalls are natural barriers. They hold trout that have migrated upstream but can't pass the falls. However, above the waterfalls is an entirely new ecosystem that holds separate trout populations that few anglers think to access.

Tree falls are great gatherers of wood debris that flow downstream in high water events. These collection areas create scours underneath them and provide cover for the trout. The water stays cooler, as it is protected from the sun, and the trout feel safer from bird predation because they are covered by wood. It is darn near impossible to get a fly to the fish, but if you can, you will be rewarded.

Riffle water is the most oxygenated water in a stream. Trout seek this habitat when water temperatures rise and start to deplete the oxygen levels. If there has been an extended warm spell and trout are not where you normally find them, try the heads of those pools in the riffle water. The advent of tight line nymphing has put a focus on fishing riffle water. The nymphs tied for tight line nymphing are ideal for running through riffle water and catching trout.

Holding pools are abnormally deep pools in a river. They are the deepest water in the particular stretch of stream you are fishing. They hold colder

Natural barriers mean wild trout.

water and are deep enough to protect fish from birds of prey. They also protect fish from predators like mink, as the fish can swim to the rocks at the bottom of the pool as soon as the prey enters the water. We like to locate these pools because many trout inhabit pools of this size and depth. It is not unusual for us to catch in excess of ten trout when we find a holding pool in one of our streams. We have noticed over the years that the largest trout in the pool is almost always the trout that hits your fly first. But we have also noticed that we catch the biggest fish in the pool last. Don't stop fishing a holding pool until all the fish stop hitting your flies.

Pocket water are those small quiet spots of water in a stream. We like the pockets that are either right in front of a boulder or directly behind a boulder in the stream. The upstream side of the boulder separates the stream, and this creates a pocket of quiet water right in front of the rock. Fish lie here and have a front seat to any food that is washing downstream. Fish don't have to work hard because the rock absorbs most of the stream energy. The other pocket is right downstream of the boulder. This pocket is usually bigger than the pocket in front of the rock. Since the rock blocks the visual of food washing downstream, fish will be at the end of the pocket. But should the fish see you, they will be under the rock before you can blink.

The final piece of water that holds fish is the seam. A seam is just like a seam on your shirt—it is a line that joins two pieces of water. Look where a smaller feeder stream joins a larger stream. There is a seam where the two waters join. The force of the two waters joining actually slows down the current. As the water mixes, it slows down and fish will sit in this area, as they don't have to work hard in that lie. They can watch for food being washed in from both stream sources.

The other seam to look for is when a larger pool will narrow and the force of the water back flows to the head of the pool. This presents two opportunities. The first is to fish the quieter water of the seam. Fish will lie in the quieter water waiting for food. It has been our experience that when flows are heavy from rain, fish will actually face downstream and look for food coming back up the slower eddy. Seams—don't forget to fish them.

Once you have fished these different water types, you will become proficient in finding where the trout hide. It takes time to learn how to read the water. If you don't get to a secret water all that often, keep a logbook. This will save you time, and each reading of your logbook will build a library of fishing facts in your brain. Let's go find some secret waters!

On the way to a secret water.

PART II

THE SECRET WATERS

The boys had a great day fishing in the Great North Woods. They caught several fine trout in the ponds where they were fishing. But there was only tomorrow morning left for fishing before they had to break camp and return to life.

"Some quick brook fishing tomorrow morning," said the Old Timer.

"It's our last chance to have trout for breakfast," said Goose, licking his lips.

"More like brunch," said Pic. "We have to check out by noon."

"Relax men," said Troutman. "We have been staying here so long that I am sure Bonnie won't mind a late checkout."

The Old Timer had already opened the New Hampshire Gazetteer. He had a couple of favorite thin blue lines that he knew held some nice native brook trout.

"Same rules as always?" asked the Old Timer.

"Two fish each, six inches," said Pic.

Everyone nodded in agreement. No one needed to eat more than two trout when brunch included eggs, bacon, home fries and English muffins. The trout were precious. There was no need to kill more than they could eat.

Troutman looked over at the Old Timer. His mind was still sharp, but he had slowed over the years. Troutman knew the Old Timer would want to hike in to an old beaver pond. But those days had passed.

"Let's hit Coon Brook," said Troutman to the Old Timer. "We haven't fished there in quite some time."

"I'd really like to hike in to…" said the Old Timer, his voice tailing off. "Coon Brook works for me."

"Goose and I will head upstream on Perry," said Pic. "We know just the place to find four nice brookies."

1

THE GREAT NORTH WOODS

BOUNDARY POND sits in the shadow of Mount D'Urban on the Canadian border. This is a fantastic mountain pond with lots of feisty brook trout. It is the headwaters of the famous Magalloway River, and you can see Canada from its waters. There is *always* wind on this pond, except during the quiet hour in the morning or the evening. A perfectly clear day can often have white caps on the pond. Strong paddling skills and a good partner make this pond a joy. Many times, we will paddle along the north shoreline and then let the wind blow us back down the pond while trolling a Light Edson Tiger Bucktail. We have caught some of our biggest trout using this method.

On the south side of the pond, about two thirds of the length of the pond, sits an old log cabin. This cabin is a last vestige of the land-lease program once run by the timber companies. It is the only structure on the pond. When we find a cabin, or a cabin cellar, on a pond, we immediately fish the waters in front of the cabin. Early visitors often placed their cabins right in front of the best water on a pond. This is true at Boundary. The shoreline drops off quickly, and trout gather in the depths waiting to pounce on baitfish or brook trout parr. Boundary Pond has a reproducing population of brook trout that is sometimes supplemented with stocked fish by New Hampshire Fish and Game.

The west end of the pond is our favorite piece of water. We can start by casting streamers, switch to wet flies and then cast to the evening hatches. Our favorite flies are Light Edson Tiger, Dark Edson Tiger, Harris Special and Supervisor. Wet flies are the "88," Professor, Heron Fly, Montreal and

East Inlet Pittsburg, New Hampshire.

Hornberg in natural and yellow. Hatches have been changing over the years on Boundary Pond. There used to be some very good mayfly hatches, but those have been sporadic the last few years. The caddis hatches are still strong, and when a good caddis hatch is on, it looks like it is raining on the pond. Dry flies we like include Elk Hair Caddis, Light Cahill, Dun Variant, Royal Wulff, White Wulff and PMX Royal.

Boundary Pond is one of the jewels in the town of Pittsburg. It is a long ride up East Inlet Road, and it is the first left after crossing over the Magalloway Brook. It's about a mile straight uphill to the parking area and then a quarter mile portage down to the pond. This is not a bad hike down, but it is a long hike back after a day of fishing. Boundary Pond is fly fishing only with a five-fish or five-pound limit. We think you should do neither. When we want breakfast trout, we fish downstream in Magalloway Brook. There are plenty of small wild trout from the outlet to the Maine border for us to enjoy in the cast iron pan. For Boundary Pond to maintain its full potential, all trout should be released immediately.

EAST INLET AND NORTON POOL PRESERVE are part of one of the large riverine bog complexes in Pittsburg. The dam and boating launch are a great place to get started on an East Inlet trouting adventure. Trout are stocked at the dam and spread out in the general area. The jewels of this water are upstream of the bog and upriver into the Norton Pool. During the spring season, it is easy to paddle up to the head of the bog, as water levels are high. As the season wears on, one must canoe along the riverbed, which can easily be followed by avoiding the marsh grasses. When moose populations are strong, East Inlet is a great place to view these magnificent creatures.

As we paddle up the inlet, we look for rock outcroppings along the shoreline. These areas usually signify spring seeps that make refuges for trout. The farther up the bog we go, the wilder the trout become. Eventually, we get into the East Inlet River. This part of the complex is filled with woody debris and the meanders that just scream wild trout. As we approach the Norton Pool, there are several places we will need to portage to keep going. This is trout fishing that approaches anything close to the wilderness that the Great North Woods are known for. We work hard, but the rewards are more than worth the effort.

In the spring, as we paddle up the bog, we troll a Mickey Finn Bucktail or a Ballou Special. These patterns will help you locate any trout in the big water. As we enter the stream complex, we'll switch over to a Little Brook Trout Bucktail or a Light Edson Tiger. When you locate trout, anchor above the pool and spend some time running streamers through the water. You will catch several trout. In summer and fall, troll a small Maynard Marvel or a larger Yellow Hornberg. Use the same techniques. For wet flies, we like to use the Professor, Montreal, Light Cahill, Dark Cahill or Parmachenee Belle. Dry fly action is sporadic but look at the alders as you paddle to Norton Pool. You can even shake the branches to see if there is a response from the trout. We have seen caddis hatches on East Inlet but nothing truly memorable. Elk Hair Caddis or the Parachute Adams in various hook sizes should cover the dry fly action.

Below the dam, the fishing can be quite memorable. When we want to put in the effort, we fish from the dam down to a logging road spur—about a mile of river. This is water where the wild trout almost never see a fly once you get past the bridge below the dam. The water is alder lined and casting is troublesome but throw short casts and feed line so that flies float down to good lies. The Hornberg is your go-to fly here. Regular, yellow or orange all work equally well.

Once you reach the logging road bridge, the East Inlet brook changes. It gets wider as it approaches Second Connecticut Lake. There is good cover and strong runs to fish here. This stretch of river is best in spring when waters are high or the end of the season when the lake-run brook trout and the occasional salmon enter the river to spawn. During these stretches, we like to use Gray Ghost, Black Ghost, Ballou Special and Muddler Minnow. While good-sized wild brook trout inhabit this section of the river all season long, do not be surprised if the fish on the end of the line is a memory maker.

The East Inlet Road leads us to these waters. It is a well-maintained dirt road, and travel is fine with any type of vehicle. We like to throw the canoe on our four-wheel drive pickup so that we are prepared for any condition we may incur.

CONNECTICUT RIVER BETWEEN THIRD AND SECOND LAKE has the potential to be a destination wild brook trout fishery. While this portion of the river is close to Route 3, it is not easy to access. This toughness protects the trout and makes it exciting to fish. The only thing keeping this section of river from greatness is the Moose Falls Flowage. The dam that creates the flowage is top release, so the water in the flowage heats up in the summer and raises the temperature in the river to inhospitable temperatures. The dam also blocks fish passage, and the lake-run fish that move up the river to spawn in the fall get blocked by the dam. There have been many Falls when we caught beautiful lake-run fish at the base of the dam. If those fish ever get the opportunity to have the run of the river, then the river will reach its full potential.

Early in our fishing careers, we would hike into some of the massive beaver flowages that made up a part of the river. These flowages held large brook trout and still do today. We just need to locate them. Once we find one, we get onto the beaver dam. This will be the most open casting area. We can throw long lines with either wet or dry flies. As with all beaver flowages, the Royal Coachman is our friend. We like to have these flies as drys, wets, wulffs or stimulators. These flies are the winner for any beaver flowages all over the state but are especially effective in this portion of the Connecticut River.

From the dam down to the junction with Scott Brook, this river is a dream: great runs, good pools and large woody debris. Our minds wander to the potential greatness as we catch the small wild brook trout and the occasional salmon parr. It is a shame that such potential is wasted.

The Hornberg owns this section of river. We always catch fish with this fly here. We also like the Muddler Minnow and the Little Brook Trout Bucktail. Wet flies include the March Brown, Light Cahill and Dark Cahill. Dry flies include the Adams, Parachute Adams, Grizzly Wulff and Yellow Humpy.

The best access is at Deer Mountain Campground for water below the Moose Falls Flowage. If you want to canoe upstream, launch at the Moose

Falls Flowage. There is car top access. It is always questionable how far upstream we will get on the river. A new beaver dam can be right around any bend in the river. Portage is always an option. This river is worth the effort now. But the fishing could be so much better.

WEST INLET BROOK is a wild brook trout spot that can give you a couple of hours of fun. Because the West Inlet Brook is so small, we use our six-foot, three-weight rods, short leader and barbless wet flies. Every pool has many fish, most of which are four inches or less. They are beautiful fish, and when you hold one in your hand, you can feel just how precious these fish are as you slip them back into the water. When you suddenly get a strike from a six-inch fish, it feels like a trophy. There have been many days when West Inlet Brook has kept the skunk off our fishing trip.

UNKNOWN POND is a difficult pond to access. Many will not even try. You have to follow an old woods road off Big Brook Bog Road to access the north end of the pond. Bushwhack around the west end of the pond and enter any opening you can find. This is a float tube pond all the way. Last time we were there, we found a canoe or two stashed, but they were in poor condition. This pond is loaded with wild brook trout and any of the remote stocked trout that get air dropped by New Hampshire Fish and Game.

We like to fish this pond in the summer. The springs-fed pond stays cool, and the added elevation keeps it that way. The rocky part of the shoreline is the deepest water, and we always find trout in that location. It's too bad that this is a hike-in-hike-out pond. We have stayed as late as possible with hatches just beginning, and we need to leave, so we can get back to the vehicles before it gets pitch black.

If we go to Unknown Pond after the helicopter stocking, we start fishing with a Little Brook Trout Bucktail. The wild fish in this pond just love feasting on the defenseless hatchery trout. Otherwise, we fish with Yellow Hornbergs or Yellow Wooly Worms. The Gray Hackle and the Brown Hackle will also get a response. Once the hatches start, we try to match the size bug with either an Adams or an Elk Hair Caddis. If the fish are too finicky, we will put floatant on an "88" and fish that or a big White Wulff. This technique is good for a few trout.

It is hard work to fish this hidden gem, but it is worth it. We have never seen another individual at Unknown Pond. If you want to enjoy a wilderness trout fishing experience in Pittsburg, this is the place.

COON BROOK AND COON BROOK BOG have some of the prettiest brook trout in Pittsburg. We began fishing the brook before we were able to access the bog. Back when logging companies only made roads passable for the logging season, the road to Coon Brook Bog would only be good for a year or two before washing out. This meant that only the hardcore anglers with off-road vehicles could access the bog. This was the heyday of fishing in the bog. Once the logging companies realized it was less expensive to build a permanent road than to always rebuild the road, access to the bog was available to everyone. It didn't take long for the fishing to decline, though it is still robust with smaller fish. While Coon Brook Bog is fly fishing only, there is a five-fish limit. New Hampshire Fish and Game has flip-flopped from stocking one-year-old fish to fingerlings over the years. The bog does have holdover fish and wild fish up to twelve inches, and they know their way around, so should you hook a bigger fish, there is only a slim chance to land it before it breaks off on an underwater log.

Flies we like in the bog include the Professor, Yellow Hornberg, Yellow Wooly Worm, Soft Hackle Pheasant Tail and Hare's Ear Wet. Dry flies include the Elk Hair Caddis, Dun Variant, Royal Wulff, White Wulff and Grizzly Wulff. We fish with sink-tip lines during the day and switch to floating lines for the evening hatches.

The secret water is Coon Brook itself. The brook is two and a half miles long from the dam at the bog to Route 3. After crossing under Route 3, there is another mile of water before Coon Brook runs into First Connecticut Lake. The brook is a wild trout paradise. It is overgrown with alders. It has large woody debris that form fly-eating pools, small waterfalls and beaver flowages. In summary, the brook has it all.

We break out the shortest fly rod we own to fish the brook. We do not use a leader. We use only three feet of tippet in 5x and barbless hooks. Size fourteen flies are big here. Most of the fishing is done with wet flies and nymphs. We use Hare's Ear, Pheasant Tails, Casuals, Prince and Zug Bug for nymphs and Royal Coachmen, Brown Hackle, Gray Hackle, Orange Fish Hawk and Light Cahill for wet flies. There is minimal casting room. Get to the head of a pool and feed line to let the fly roll downstream with the current. If a fish doesn't hit the fly as it rolls through the pool, one will surely hit as you retrieve your fly. If we do not get a strike quickly, we move to the next pool.

If you only have half a day to fish, we recommend that you park your car in the parking area at the entrance to Coon Brook Road. Hike up the road until you reach a woods road on the left (about a mile). Take the woods road down to the brook and begin fishing. If you fish it correctly, it will take half the day to reach Route 3. You can then walk up the hill to your car.

EAST BRANCH OF THE DEAD DIAMOND RIVER runs down the Diamond Ridge and is a headwater stream to the Dead Diamond River, the last stream in New Hampshire that is home to the heritage strain brook trout. We like to fish the East Branch above the natural barrier Garfield Falls. The trout here are beautiful with more of a silver-gray tint than the deep black of the hemlock forests. You can tell that this is a different strain of brook trout than other brook trout you catch in Pittsburg. Above Garfield Falls has not been stocked in decades. All hatchery characteristics have been bred out of these trout. Hook into an eight-inch trout, and you will think you have a bigger fish. We have hooked these trout on our three-weight rods and had them run down and up the pool several times.

This is a freestone stream with lots of woody debris. Long riffle runs and deep plunge pools all hold these feisty trout. You can fish upstream from the Magalloway Road bridge. Every twist and turn of the river will bring new water and pull you upstream. We especially like to visit this stream in the fall after a period of rain. The fish will move upstream as they seek out spawning water and mating partners. This brings out the bigger fish (ten inches).

Since we fish this mostly in the fall, we like to fish small streamer patterns, such as Mickey Finn, Red and White Bucktail, Edson Tigers, Little Brook Trout Bucktail or big wet fly patterns, including Olive Wooly Bugger, Yellow Hornberg, Royal Coachman, Silver Prince and Wickham's Fancy. We tie these on barbless hooks or make sure the barbs are pinched down. These trout should be released if possible.

You can reach the East Branch by traveling east on the Magalloway Road off Route 3. Follow the signs to Garfield Falls and take a left by the river and go over the bridge. Park off the roadway, as there are typically logging operations going on in that part of the forest.

ROUND POND BROOK is the outlet brook for Round Pond. At one point in time, Round Pond held a self-sustaining wild brook trout fishery. It was a fun pond to fish. Those days are not returning anytime in the future. Round Pond is dependent on the stocking truck, but Round Pond Brook is not. It still holds a great wild strain of brook trout that are fun to catch. As with all of the smaller wild brook trout brooks in Pittsburg, Round Pond Brook is overgrown and a challenge for the fly angler. Get out your shortest fly rod, short leader and colorful wet flies. Round Pond Brook will challenge you in every way possible.

There are three places we like to fish Round Pond Brook. First is from the outlet to the pond. This brook travels more than a mile and a half before crossing Route 3. When we fish the outlet stream portion, we go downstream for approximately an hour and then fish back up the brook. We can't imagine trying to bushwhack the entire mile and a half of the brook.

Our next point of entry is at the Route 3 crossing. Here we either fish upstream for an hour and then fish back downstream or we get in the brook below Route 3 and fish to Camp Otter Road. This can be done in a reasonable time period. Our final entry point, if we have permission, is to fish from Camp Otter Road down to the lake. We only undertake this trip in the spring. The mouth of Round Pond Brook can hold some very nice brook trout over a pound right after ice out. These brook trout chase the smelt that are looking for a place to spawn. This property is all privately held, so please try to get permission from a landowner before you attempt to fish this lower section of Round Pond Brook.

We fish the great streamer patterns on the lower portion of the river, including Gray Ghost, Black Ghost, Supervisor, Light Edson Tiger and

Connecticut Lakes have wild areas.

Ballou Special. In the remainder of the stream, we fish old-school wet flies, such as Royal Coachman, Parmachenee Belle, Silver Doctor, Campbell's Fancy and Queen of the Waters.

The outlet to Round Pond can be found at the end of Round Pond Road off Route 3. Camp Otter Road is approximately a mile and a half north on Route 3. Please remember to park off all travel portions of the roadways.

THE PERRY PONDS are tucked away in a corner of the Connecticut Lakes Natural Area at the headwaters to Perry Stream. As we drive up Day Road to reach the parking area for the Perry Ponds, we cross over Perry Stream several times. There are many inviting spots to stop and throw a fly but resist the temptation. A trip into the Perry Ponds is a full-day adventure without a minute to spare. In addition to the half-hour drive to the parking area after leaving Route 3, we have a mostly uphill hike of more than two miles to reach the cabin on the first pond, Lower Perry Pond. As we mentioned with Boundary Pond, where a cabin is located is the most productive part of the pond. There is deeper cooler water from the cabin and straight across the pond from that point.

To go to Upper Perry Pond, there is a trail from the north end of Lower Perry. Last time we were there it was an old skidder road, but that may have changed. We are confident that you will be able to find the trail to get to the upper pond.

Our favorite of the Perry Ponds is Wright Pond. The trail to Wright Pond breaks away from the main trail just before we reach Lower Perry Pond. It is just the perfect size to float tube, and it has a good quantity of hungry trout. There is some deeper water where the trail ends at the pond and there is the outlet at the far end of the pond. Lazily kicking and casting as we work our way down the pond is an enjoyable way to spend our time in pursuit of eager trout.

As with the majority of our float tube fishing, we use nine-foot rods. For these ponds, we like four-weight or five-weight rods. We pack in a floating line with a nine-foot leader and a sink-tip line with a seven-and-a-half-foot leader. We start with the sink-tip line and switch once there is consistent surface activity. Flies for the sink-tip include Black Wooly Bugger, Humongous, Hornberg, Harris Special, the "88" and Maynard's Marvel. Dry flies are the Adams, Royal Wulff, White Wulff, Elk Hair Caddis, Renegade and Griffth Gnat. Wet flies are Brown Hackle, Gray Hackle, Royal Coachman, Har's Ear Wet and Yellow Sparkle Hackle. We use the wet flies with either the sink-tip or the floating line.

The Perry Ponds are not easy to access. Leave plenty of time to hike in, hydrate, nap and eat lunch. This is an all-day fishing trip. The first time we hiked in, we thought we would just fish the evening hatch. We only had an hour to fish before we had to turn around and hike back to the car.

When we want to fish a wilderness pond that doesn't involve the whole day, we hike to **HARRIS POND**. Harris Pond is a fairly short walk, less than a mile, up a muddy woods road that is mostly impassable for ordinary off-road vehicles. Even in the driest of years, we have had to hike in to Harris Pond. You will see where off-road vehicles have tried and failed to drive up to this pond. There is plenty of room to park your vehicle at the start of the Harris Pond road. The parking is located almost immediately after the turn onto Shatney Road from Back Lake Road.

The two differences in Harris Pond are the size—three acres—and the depth of the water. Harris drops as deep as sixteen feet, and this is the spot where we want to concentrate on fishing. We always start with our sinking line when we start to fish the pond. When we enter the pond in our float tube, we kick straight out from where we launched. When we get about halfway across the pond, there is a change in water clarity. This is the drop-off to sixteen feet. We use our sinking lines and do the countdown method until we find fish.

Flies we like to fish in Harris Pond include the Little Brook Trout (especially after aerial stocking), Yellow Hornberg, Edson Tigers, Conehead Wooly Bugger, Harris Special, Soft Hackle Hare's Ear, Soft Hackle Pheasant Tail, Brown Hackle and Yellow Wooly Worm. Since this is a hike-in pond, we rarely fish the hatches at night. If you choose to stay and hike out with a headlamp, we recommend the Elk Hair Caddis, Royal Coachman, White Wulff, Light Cahill, Hendrickson and Parachute Adams.

INDIAN STREAM can be reached by staying on Shatney Road until it reaches Jesse Young Road. You can then follow the road all the way to the headwater streams. We enjoy fishing for the wild brook trout in the east branch, middle branch or west branch above Terrell Pond. These are the streams that feed wild brook trout to Indian Stream. There are deep plunge pools, riffle runs and pocket water that hold these feisty trout. This far up the watershed, you will need your short, three-weight rod, as some of the pools are very tight for casting. As we fish down the river, Indian Stream does open up, and casting to the brook trout is a joy.

As we work our way down Jesse Young Road, there are several feeder streams that supply cooler water to Indian Stream. We like to fish where

Roaring Brook, Graham Brook, Moose Brook, Shoppe Brook and Perry Brook enter the river. These thermal habitats will hold willing trout throughout the summer. The trout are ravenous for dry flies. In our fly box we have the Royal Wulff, White Wulff, Grizzly Wulff, Adams, Quill Gordon, Elk Hair Caddis, Renegade and Klinkhammer. We have these flies in several hook sizes, starting with size eight and going down to size eighteen. When we fish with the larger flies, we like to add a dropper fly to double our chances. Dropper flies to consider include Pheasant Tail Nymph, Hare's Ear Nymph, Zug Bug, Prince, Hendrickson Nymph or Light Cahill Nymph. We tie nymphs one hook size smaller than the dry fly hook size.

There is so much water to cover on Indian Stream that it is hard to decide where to start and where to end. We always seem to head upstream, as the more effort that you expend typically means that the hoards will not be there. However, Indian Stream does curve away from the roadway in several locations, so check the map and choose to fish those pieces of water. You will enjoy catching these fish.

A word about Terrel Pond. For many years we fished Terrell Pond, and it was regularly stocked by New Hampshire Fish and Game. But over the last decade, the pond has changed. Silt has begun to fill in the pond. This has made the pond shallower and has led to the pond heating up to levels

#gobarbless.

uninhabitable for trout. The dam that forms the pond is a top-release dam, so in the summer, Terrell Pond becomes a thermal polluter of the West Branch of Indian Stream. This is to the detriment of the wild trout downstream of the dam. We hope that one day Terrell Pond Dam will be removed, and the West Branch of Indian Stream will return to its former glory.

BACK LAKE BROOK has saved many a fishing trip to Pittsburg. The brook leaves the northwest end of Back Lake and meanders under the shadow of Shatney Mountain. It runs under Route 3 just outside of the town of Pittsburg and empties into the Connecticut River below Murphy Dam. This brook is another sleeper when it comes to catching wild brook trout. It also demands your three-weight rod. We use the standard wet flies when we fish Back Lake Brook—Royal Coachman, Parmachenee Belle, Silver Doctor, Montreal, Black Wooly Worm and Gray Hackle.

There are two places we like to fish Back Lake Brook. The first is at the bottom of the hill just past the transfer station heading south. We park off the road and either fish upstream or downstream for about an hour. This is fun little brookie fishing with wet flies. We do not actually throw a cast on this brook unless we find a fresh beaver flowage, and then we may get to roll cast. The trout are feisty, and we catch a good number of fish bigger than four inches. But an eight-inch trout is a trophy in this water.

The other spot we like to fish is above where the brook goes under Route 3. It seems that the farther downstream you get on Back Lake Brook, the bigger the fish. We will bushwhack up the brook until we find a beaver flowage or the terrain gets too marshy, and then we fish our way back to Route 3. It is a blast to fish this brook, and we should probably fish it more than we do. There are so many choices in Pittsburg and not enough time.

CARR POND is located south of Lake Francis in Clarksville. This pond is spring fed and produces some excellent species of brook trout. There is some natural reproduction in this pond, and it also receives an annual enhancement of fingerling trout from New Hampshire Fish and Game. This is a remote hike-in pond, and while we prefer to use float tubes, the trail to the pond is manageable enough to bring in a canoe with a set of transport wheels. The hike-in from the parking area is approximately a mile so carrying in a canoe is for the younger crowd. In the past, there were those who would snowmobile in a canoe in the winter and leave it at the pond. It is our understanding that this is no longer allowed as part of the Connecticut Lakes Natural Area Management Plan.

Nice parr markings of this brookie.

Carr Pond is only eleven acres, which makes getting around the pond relatively easy. Because this pond is shallow—six feet at the deepest points—we fish with sink-tip lines and floating lines. Flies we like to start with include the Light Edson Tiger, Dark Edson Tiger, Harris Special and "88." After the New Hampshire Fish and Game aerial stocking, we use the Little Brook Trout Bucktail. Wet flies we use are the Hornberg, Yellow Hornberg, Yellow Wooly Worm, Black Wooly Worm, Hare's Ear and Pheasant Tail. When the hatches are on, we use the Grizzly Wulff, White Wulff, PMX Royal, Quill Gordon, Light Cahill and Elk Hair Caddis.

We have found Carr Pond to be a feast-or-famine pond. When the fish are on the feed, the action can be nonstop. When the fish are not on the feed, we need to work really hard to catch. The nice part about float tubing Carr Pond is that you can feel the spring holes as you kick over them. We try to get twenty feet or so past a spring, and then we will cast to that spot, letting the fly sink to the bottom. Many times, we will get a strike just as the fly is approaching the surface for another cast, so be prepared.

Carr Pond can be reached off Cedar Stream Road at the east end of Lake Francis. Take a right and then another right and start looking for an old log yard that now serves as the trailhead. The walk in is relatively flat, and the trail is well marked. This makes it easy to walk out at dark after you have fished the evening hatch.

SHEHAN FLOWAGE marks the start of the Little Dead Diamond River. Shehan was formed by a dam and served as a log yard in its early years. This pond grew huge brook trout—some exceeding three pounds. As with most ponds that are general law, those fish are no longer available, and Shehan Pond relies on New Hampshire Fish and Game to supplement the natural reproduction in the pond with aerial stocking. We still catch trout up to sixteen inches in Shehan Pond, but they are the exception and not the rule.

Getting to Shehan Pond is an adventure unto itself. The road into the parking area is not marked. It is off Cedar Stream Road, and if you reach Judd Ponds, you went too far. Shehan Flowage is in the Connecticut Lake Management area, and the road into Shehan is not allowed to be maintained. We have not been into Shehan in a couple of years, and the road was barely passable with four-wheel drive at that time. It may be impassable now. This will add more than half a mile to your hike to the pond. When we arrive at the parking area next to a camp, we walk to the launch point through a quarter mile of swamp with boards and pallets to get through the wettest parts of the trail. We launch our canoe at the west end of the pond.

Shehan is twenty acres of prime trout water. Deadfalls and stumpage are everywhere and so are the trout. We start fishing almost immediately and cast to the structure as we paddle down the pond to the deeper water. As you are catching trout, you will notice that some trout look different in shape and coloring. This is due to the difference in the wild brook trout when compared to the fingerling trout flown in from the hatchery. If any of the hatchery fish survive, you will notice that they are not as robust as the wild native fish that reproduce in Shehan.

Because of the structure in the bottom of Shehan, we use sink-tip lines. This gives us better control of where our flies are fishing and keeps lost flies to a minimum. That being said, if we aren't losing flies, then we aren't fishing deep enough in the pond. Shehan was the pond where we learned about fishing the Little Brook Trout Bucktail. We were there one weekend right after the aerial stocking and saw all these fingerling trout in and around the deadfalls. They were laying in the sunny warmer water, and all of a sudden, a big trout would cruise through and gobble up a fingerling. We immediately put on the Little Brook Trout Bucktail and caught larger trout on almost every cast.

Streamers that work for Shehan include the Little Brook Trout Bucktail, Red and White Bucktail, Edson Tigers, Harris Special, Maynard Marvel and White Marabou. Wet flies we like are the Montreal, "88," Professor, Muddler, Hornberg and Yellow Hornberg. Dry flies are the Elk Hair Caddis, Quill Gordon, Hendrickson, Light Cahill, Renegade and Royal Wulff.

Frankly, we hope Shehan Pond Road is unpassable. Then Shehan Pond would have a chance to return to its former glory.

The JUDD PONDS are just up around the corner from Shehan Pond Road. If the fishing has been slow on Shehan or if it looks like a storm may be approaching, we will fish the Judd Ponds. The Judd Ponds are small spring-fed ponds that eventually empty into the Dead Diamond Rivers. You can see the ponds from Cedar Stream Road, and it is an easy hike down to the ponds with either a float tube or a canoe. Because the ponds are smaller, we typically opt for the float tubes.

The Judds also receive a fingerling stocking. Since these ponds are small and only hold smaller trout, we do wonder why they get these hatchery trout. There was natural reproduction in the past, but these ponds are also general law with a five-fish limit, so over harvest must take a toll on the Judds.

We mostly dry-fly fish the Judds. It is small and the trout are willing. We prefer to use any of the Wulff Flies in sizes fourteen down to eighteen. We catch some trout and enjoy a couple of hours just floating around and landing fish. It is a great alternative if we don't feel the need to put the effort into Shehan or if it looks like the weather may change for the worse sooner rather than later.

NATHAN POND is a great wilderness experience in one of the wildest, harshest places in New Hampshire, Dixville Notch. Sheer granite walls, deep valleys and lung-burning hiking trails—with land this rugged, you know the inhabitants are rugged as well. This rings true for the brook trout in Nathan Pond. When we choose to hike to Nathan Pond, it is an experience we do not soon forget. The hiking trail is approximately two and a half miles from Pond Brook Road. While the trail follows the valley that holds Nathan Pond Brook, it is uphill all the way. With a float tube on our back, it is an effort to reach the pond—but so worth it.

Nathan Pond is twenty-two acres and more than twenty feet deep. This is a habitat that holds big trout. We love to fish big flies with sinking lines in Nathan Pond, and we dredge the deep water to catch big brook trout. We fish fast-sink lines with seven-and-a-half-foot leaders with 3x tippets. When we hook up with the trout of a lifetime, we do not want to lose that fish.

We start by fishing the boulders along the shoreline of the outlet and then work to the deeper waters. This pond demands that we use the countdown method of fishing and make sure we fish the clock. We start at the twelve o'clock position and move clockwise in our tube. We start with a five count and proceed from there. We have to cover as much water as we can so that we can find the trout. Once we find the trout, we are sure to have smiles on our faces.

We like to use the more modern streamers in Nathan Pond. These have added weight and help you to get deep fast. The Complex Twist Bugger, Rubber Leg Bugger, Fish Skull Bugger and Senyo Trout Parr will help in your search for the big one. Once we locate the trout, we can switch to the more tried and true patterns like the Gray Ghost, Black Ghost or Edson Tigers. This pond is also aerial stocked, so don't forget to fish the Little Brook Trout Bucktail in shallower water if you get to Nathan Pond after that stocking.

Sadly, an ATV trail was added that comes near Nathan Pond. This has made Nathan an easy target for the general law fisherman, and we have noticed a decline in the number of large trout we have caught. Hopefully, New Hampshire Fish and Game will notice this decline and include Nathan Pond in its Quality Trout Program.

You can see trout from up high.

The **Magalloway River** is the last remaining home for big wild river brook trout in New Hampshire. Each year, trout that exceed five pounds are caught in the New Hampshire portion of the Magalloway River. These trout travel extensively throughout the watershed and have been found to travel up into the Diamond River System to spawn and into the Androscoggin River to winter over. Some of these fish have even been tracked into the Rapid River in Maine. These trout are very hard to locate, and timing is very important. These big fish do not hang in any one spot very long.

That being said, we will share our one spot that we try for these fish. There is a very small portion of the Magalloway River that enters New Hampshire from Maine. The river is joined by the Swift Diamond River. The river quickly goes back into Maine. We access this portion of the river by canoe from the Route 16 crossing in Maine and float down the river until we reach the next Route 16 crossing in Maine. If you do not have a Maine fishing license, be very careful. This section of the river is patrolled extensively by both New Hampshire and Maine conservation officers. They don't take breaking the rules lightly.

Fishing here should be strictly barbless hooks and catch and release. Play these fish quickly. That is why we use 3x tippets. We also use six-weight or seven-weight fly rods. Flies need to be *big*. Start at size four and work up from there. Use a clear rubber catch and release net. Take one picture, preferably with the fish in the net in the water, and then send the fish back home quickly.

Regulations to protect these trout are constantly changing. Please check the current regulations before you venture to the river. These trout are too valuable to be caught only once.

Whitcomb Pond is a remote pond in the Nash Stream Forest. The Nash Stream Forest is one of the nicest forest tracks in New Hampshire. Home to Nash Stream, a wild brook trout water, we tend to focus more on the ponds in this area of the state. Easiest access to the Nash Stream Forest is from Route 110 in Stark and onto the Nash Stream Road. You will reach a trailhead for the Trio Ponds Trail. Whitcomb is a remote pond that is fun to float tube and fish. This pond receives an aerial stocking of fingerling trout and has some natural reproduction as well.

Whitcomb is more than 2,200 feet in elevation. Coupled with the springs in the pond, this means cool water for the trout all season long. You don't have to worry about finding spring holes or overstressing trout in this fine pond. We like to take our sink tip and our floating fly lines into Whitcomb Pond. As is our way, we start with the sink-tip lines and dredge streamers

Plunge pool inhabitant.

and wet flies. This helps us locate the fish. We try smaller-sized streamers like the Warden's Worry, Ballou Special, Mickey Finn and Red and White. If these don't draw a strike, then we try the wet flies, Hornberg, Casual, "88," Professor or Montreal.

This is not a bad hike-in pond, so we can stay for the dry-fly action. In Whitcomb, we find matching the size of the pattern is more important than matching the hatch. In our fly box, we will have the Adams, Parachute Adams, Quill Gordon and Elk Hair Caddis in a variety of hook sizes. Once we have the correct size fly, we can enjoy the fishing.

The **TRIO PONDS** are the next water we fish in the Nash Stream Forest. The lesser-known and lesser-fished Upper Trio Pond is smaller and shallower than its cousin Lower Trio Pond. Both ponds receive aerial stockings from New Hampshire Fish and Game. There is also some natural reproduction in these ponds. We have fished the Upper Trio Pond a couple of times, but the Lower Trio Pond is the one that calls to us. It is bigger and deeper and has larger trout available to the fly fisher.

In Upper Trio Pond, we fish sink-tips and wet flies for the smallish trout, using Brown Hackle, Gray Hackle, Wooly Worm, Hornberg, Royal Coachman and Silver Prince. The trout are anxious to grab your fly. You will enjoy jousting with these fish. The larger trout we find are near the deep hole at the north end of the pond. For the most part, this is a quantity over quality pond, but it is a lot of fun.

Lower Trio Pond is where we spend the most time fishing. Lower Trio is big by float tube standards, at sixty acres. It is also very deep for its size, thirty-five feet. To know where to start fishing on Lower Trio Pond, just look for the cabins. They are located on the lower end of the pond and are across from the deepest part of the pond. Start with a sinking line and do the countdown method until fish are located. We may have to kick quite a bit of the pond to find fish, but when we do, we are in luck.

We have caught trout larger than sixteen inches in Lower Trio Pond, and the water says there should be bigger specimens available—we just haven't caught them yet. Start with streamers, Gray Ghost, Black Ghost, Warden's Worry, Edson Tigers and Muddler Minnow. If the fish are biting when we are at Lower Trio, we get multiple strikes. We don't really bother with wet flies or nymphs here. We are always looking for the big fish, and that means casting big flies.

We are sure there is dry-fly fishing to be had at the Trio Ponds, we just have not taken the time to fish there for the hatches. It is definitely a big trout or go home type of pond for us.

A word about LITTLE BOG POND. We usually skip right by Little Bog Pond. The other ponds are simply too productive for us to fish this water. We have learned recently that there is some stocking of larger hatchery fish taking place in Little Bog Pond, and this is good for two reasons. First, it will take some of the fishing pressure off the Trio Ponds and Whitcomb Pond. Second, it will be a lot less frustrating to beginning anglers who are trying to catch a brook trout in a wilderness setting. Perhaps the next time we are in the Nash Stream Forest we will give Little Bog Pond a try.

LONG POND in Millsfield is another remote New Hampshire trout pond. It is a twenty-eight-acre pond that is spring-fed with an average depth of five feet. This makes it ideal for float tubing. This pond receives an aerial stocking from New Hampshire Fish and Game, so there are plenty of trout to pursue. We have found that when the bite is on, you can catch trout anywhere on the pond. Because the pond is shallow, it doesn't suffer from high winds and waves, and kicking around the pond is a delight.

The shallowness of this pond means we start the fishing with our sink-tip lines and seven-and-a-half-foot leaders. The trout we catch here are on the smaller side, so we fish smaller flies when we begin fishing. We like

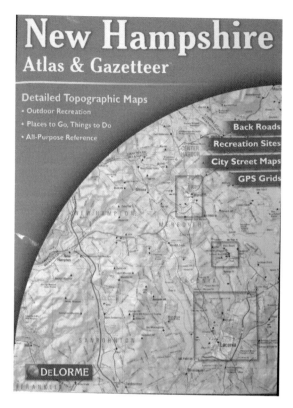

Delorme Atlas is your friend.

to use the Hornberg, Yellow Hornberg, Harris Special and Light Edson Tiger. If these flies don't bring a response, we switch to wet flies. The Yellow Wooly Worm, Professor, Parmachenee Belle and Montreal can bring a response.

Cratered between Signal Mountain and Mount Patience, this is a classic North Woods pond. You can reach Long Pond off Millsfield Pond Road. We can usually count on seeing various wildlife species as we kick around the pond. One time, we were fishing along the western shoreline, and a whitetail doe came down to the water with a fawn in tow to get a drink. It was a picture-postcard moment. When a hatch commences, the pond looks like it is raining. We use any of the usual dry flies for the trout on Long Pond, including Wulff Flies, Adams, Dun Variant and Elk Hair Caddis. We have these in a variety of sizes, and we have success with them.

If we have time before we leave the pond, or if we want to stretch our legs during a float tube break, we will fish the outlet brook to Long Pond. The brook is usually good for a few wild brook trout.

Moose Pond is another of our Millsfield Ponds that we fish when we are in the area. Moose Pond is one of those ponds that just feels right when you are on the water. At twenty-nine acres, this is a great pond to use the float tube, but you can carry a canoe in as well. When we fish Moose Pond, we will kick our way over the inlet from Rock Pond. The cooler water can be a draw for trout. If that is unsuccessful, we will kick our float tube out from the inlet and fish the deep hole. Remember our remote pond mantra: look for the cabins, and that is the best place to start fishing.

This pond is not that deep, so we start with our sink-tip line on a four-weight or five-weight rod. We use a seven-foot leader to fish our wet flies and a nine-foot leader to fish our dry flies. Streamers we like are the Mickey Finn, Black Ghost, Humungus, Muddler, Wooly Bugger and Hornberg. We use the countdown method to find the right depth for the fish when we are at Moose Pond. Typically, this is around the deep spot in the elbow of the pond.

When a hatch breaks out, matching the size of the fly is more important than the color. Dry flies are Quill Gordon, Hendrickson, Light Cahill, Royal Wulff, Adams and Elk Hair Caddis. Have these flies in sizes from twelve to sixteen, and you will have success.

We reach Moose Pond by taking Twitchell Road from Millsfield Pond Road. If we have time or the fishing on Moose Pond is slow, we take a hike into Rock Pond. Rock Pond has the structure and the depth to hold wild brook trout. We only had about an hour to spend on Rock Pond, but we will be returning and investing more time to locate the trout.

The west branch of Clear Stream is the brook that we fish when visiting Millsfield. We can take the access road from Route 26 and drive until we reach the bridge that crosses the brook. We then take out our three-weight rod set up and jump into the stream. This is some fun wild brook trout fishing. Due to the proximity of the road, you can fish as far down the west branch as you like and then bushwhack out to the road and return to the car.

This is short-leader fishing with our favorite wet flies. We sometimes use just three feet of tippet. Flies that we like to fish the west branch with are Royal Coachman, Montreal, Professor, Gray Hackle, Brown Hackle and Wooly Worm. It is a fun way to hit the water and catch a few wild brook trout before going to your next fishing destination.

DUSTAN POND is a remote water located in Wentworths Location. This pond is the hardest of the Wentworths Location ponds to access. It is a hike-in from the Skyway Trail. Dustan Pond is only five acres, making it an ideal float tube pond, especially with the hike-in component.

The two places we like to fish in Dustan Pond are the inlet on the west shore and the outlet that sends Greenough Brook into Little Greenough Pond. Dustan is a shallow pond, so sink-tip and floating lines are the choice. We start with the Hornberg, Yellow Hornberg, Black Wooly Worm, Yellow Wooly Worm, Brown Hackle, Gray Hackle and the sink-tip line. We use the countdown method to find the depth for the fish. Once we have located the fish, it's game on. Dry flies on floating lines include Royal Wulff, Royal Stimulator, PMX Royal, Elk Hair Caddis, Yellow Humpy and Doodle Bug.

If we fish Dustan Pond after New Hampshire Fish and Game does the aerial stocking, the Little Brook Trout Bucktail is the fly of choice—the aerial stocking is like a dinner bell for the larger trout in Dustan Pond. If you want to have a chance at the larger fish, we think this is the best time to give it a try.

Look at those fins.

LITTLE BEAR BROOK POND is the next pond in Wentworths Location to fish for wild brook trout. This is a five-acre pond, making it ideal for float tube fishing. Due to the small size of this pond, we can fish it in an afternoon. We target the structure along the edges of the pond and have found the east shore to be most productive.

When we hike to Little Bear Brook Pond during the day, we start with a sink-tip line, using little streamers or wet flies in size ten or twelve. Streamers include Muddler, Mickey Finn, Supervisor, Black Ghost Marabou and Red and White Bucktail. The Little Brook Trout Bucktail is the fly we use after the aerial stocking by New Hampshire Fish and Game. Wet flies are Hornberg, Yellow Hornberg, Hendrickson, Light Cahill, Parmachenee Belle and Hare's Ear.

We have never seen another angler on this pond. When we want a remote pond experience with a feeling like we are back in the early 1900s, we think that Little Bear Brook Pond fills that desire.

LITTLE GREENOUGH POND is a wild brook trout pond. This pond is not stocked by New Hampshire Fish and Game. This pond is a barbless-hook, catch-and-release pond. It closes on Labor Day so the trout can spawn without interruption. Little Greenough Pond is the poster child for what brook trout fishing could be in New Hampshire if we protect the habitat and the fish.

Little Greenough Pond is a big brook trout pond. Every time you visit the pond, you have a chance for the fish of a lifetime. Trout up to three pounds are possible. These fish are gorgeous. They are defiantly a strain of fish that is different than other brook trout that you find around the state. If it wasn't so much effort to reach Little Greenough, we would fish it all the time. It is just that amazing of a pond.

Little Greenough Pond is forty-two acres, so we like to canoe, though you can float tube. You will get a workout trying to get around this pond by kicking. Since we like big brook trout, we fish big flies in Little Greenough. Don't use anything with a hook size smaller than six. We use Muddler, Little Brook Trout Bucktail, Gray Ghost and Humungous—anything to temp these trout into attacking.

The one time we dry fly fish Little Greenough is during the hexagenia hatch. These big mayflies bring big trout to the surface. There is nothing more exciting than a large brook trout inhaling a size six dry fly, trust us. We won't divulge our favorite spots on this pond. Half the fun was learning them ourselves. We know that you will enjoy it too.

Little Greenough Pond can be found off Greenough Pond Road that leaves Route 16 in Errol.

GREENOUGH POND is the last great trout pond in Wentworths Location. At 234 acres, this pond is bigger than most of the waters that we fish. Greenough Pond gives us two opportunities that we don't normally have: fly fishing for lake trout and trolling tandem streamers. There is a car top boat launch, and motors are allowed. This is great for trolling after the ice goes out of Greenough Pond and the road gets opened to vehicular traffic.

When trolling, we like to take a fly reel and put on a lead core line. The lead core line gets our fly down to where the fish are located. Lead core line changes color every ten feet, which allows the angler to know how deep they are when they catch a fish. Because of the weight of a lead core line, we like to troll with a seven- or eight-weight fly rod. This will handle the pull of the lead core line. A rod at these weights will also be able to handle any fish that are measured in pounds, not inches. Lake trout are plentiful in Greenough Pond, so we won't really know what we have on the end of our line until it comes to the surface. Tandem flies (a fly with two hooks) we use are the Gray Ghost, Red Gray Ghost, Nine Three, Supervisor and Barnes Special.

When we want to catch our lake trout by casting, we paddle (motors disrupt the wilderness setting) over to either of the two inlets—one from Little Greenough and one from Dustan Pond. These waters tend to warm faster than the remainder of Greenough Pond, and the bait fish the lake trout crave congregate at these locations. We anchor our canoe and cast the clock looking for cruising trout. We aren't surprised when we catch a brook trout instead of a lake trout. We use the same flies as trolling but use a single hook casting streamer. One additional fly to add is the Little Brook Trout Bucktail, as brook trout fry get washed into Greenough Pond from either of the inlet brooks.

WENTWORTHS LOCATION packs more big trout punch for the pound than any other township in New Hampshire. This small township has three great

Many hike-in locations allow camping.

remote trout ponds and a large great pond. If you want to keep travel to a minimum and fish from sunrise to sunset, Wentworths Location is the place. The majority of the land in Wentworths Location has been protected from development by land purchases from a combination of state, land trusts and private landowner partnerships.

ROUND POND in Errol is a fun little water to chase brook trout. While there is some natural reproduction, New Hampshire Fish and Game stocks the pond with fingerling trout to help the pressure from those anglers who like to take trout home. Round Pond is forty-two acres with a depth of less than ten feet. This pond is loaded with springs. Finding the spring holes and focusing on those fish is the challenge for success.

We like to start with our sink tip lines and streamer patterns. The Light Edson Tiger, Humungous, Marabou Black Ghost or Black Wooly Bugger are good searching patterns. We use the countdown method to find where the trout are located. As it is only forty-two acres, Round Pond is just small enough to use a float tube. The pond is cartop boat accessible, so we like to use our canoe. This makes it easier to cover the pond by trolling our streamer, and once we start to catch fish, we can anchor and fish that location.

Fishing with our sink-tip line, we change over to our favorite wet flies. Round Pond fishes well using the Hornberg, Yellow Hornberg, Harris Special, Maynard Marvel, Professor, "88" and Wooly Worm. We will concentrate on an area for thirty minutes to an hour and then resume trolling around the pond.

Hatches for dry fly fishing include Quill Gordon, Light Cahill, Mosquito, White Wulff, PMX Royal, Dun Variant and Parachute Adams. As with the majority of our dry fly fishing, we try to match the size of the bugs, not necessarily the color. If a cahill hatch starts, try to match the size of the bug and then get as close as you can to the color.

While not one of the wildest of locations in the Great North Woods, Round Pond is easy to access and a lot of fun to fish when the bite is on. We rarely see another angler here.

Two ponds that are close to each other are SWEAT POND and SIGNAL POND. Both are remote hike-in ponds. They have natural reproducing populations of brook trout, and they both receive supplemental stockings of fingerlings from New Hampshire Fish and Game. While they are both in the shadow of Signal Mountain, no two ponds could fish any differently.

Sweat Pond is ten acres and is perfect for your float tube. The reason we like this pond is the deep drop-off in the southern end of the pond. If there is a recipe for big brook trout, this is it. We use sinking lines in this pond and focus exclusively on seeking out the bigger fish. It is not unusual to catch trout over twelve inches in Sweat Pond. The fish don't come easy, but they are just too beautiful to pass up.

As with many of our aerial stocked ponds, we try to fish Sweat Pond within a week to ten days of the stocking. We fish Little Brook Trout Bucktails as the bigger trout have answered the dinner bell and feed almost exclusively on these hatchery trout. If you can't wait until the aerial stocking, we like to fish bucktails and streamers on our sinking line. The Black Ghost, Edson Tiger (light and dark), Supervisor, Muddler and Warden's Worry will catch trout early in the season.

When we fish after the stocking, we like to use soft hackles and emergers with a floating line and long leaders, including Pheasant Tail, Hare's Ear, Brown Hackle, Gray Hackle, Sparkle Emerger and Fripple. These flies fished just under the surface will bring strikes before the hatches begin at dusk.

We have not spent enough time on Sweat Pond to have the hatches dialed in. We usually walk back out before it gets too dark. The hike-in is one of our longer hikes, so we don't get a chance to take advantage of the dry fly fishing here. We suspect that the usual Great North Woods dry flies will work as well here as they do at other ponds. We recommend the Royal Wulff, White Wulff, Grizzly Wulff, PMX Royal, Dun Variant and Elk Hair Caddis. If the bigger fish hit dry flies the way they hit bucktails, you will be in for the time of your life.

Signal Pond is almost the opposite of Sweat Pond. It is small—five acres—and not very deep. The average depth is only three feet. There is a deep spot in the north end of the pond but not the twenty foot depth like Sweat Pond. The small size makes Signal Pond ideal for the float tube angler.

The fish in Signal seem to be more like wild brook trout, and they act accordingly. We fish Signal Pond with sink-tip lines or floating lines with fluorocarbon leaders. There is a good amount of insect life in Signal Pond. We like to start fishing with our wet flies and soft hackles. We use Professor, Parmachenee Belle, Campbell's Fancy, Silver Prince, Montreal and Silver Doctor for old-school wet flies and Orange Fish Hawk, Brown Hackle, Gray Hackle, Partridge and Yellow and Sparkle Soft Hackle for emerger patterns. If these don't draw a response, go to the old standby, the Hornberg.

Hatches react accordingly, so bring the Royal Wulff, White Wulff, Dun Variant, Quill Gordon, Adams Parachute and Elk Hair Caddis. Remember to match the size before trying to match the color.

It is fun to follow the outlet brook from Signal Pond into the woods and catch little wild brook trout. There have been times when the slow fishing in Signal Pond was saved by some fast action in the brook. Take out your old-school wet flies and enjoy some fast action with these beautiful, wild fish.

We have learned that there are now ATV trails that can take you close to these two ponds. We hope that the easier access doesn't destroy these two fisheries. We have enjoyed fishing here over the years (despite the effort) and hope that you will have a chance to enjoy it as well.

MUNN POND is the sleeper pond in the town of Errol. It isn't that far off Route 16. It isn't too big for a canoe or float tube and isn't too small that you feel like you are wasting time. The walk-in is just long enough that you aren't exhausted. And the trout are *amazing*.

Make no mistake, Munn Pond is a *big* brook trout pond—it is more than thirty feet deep, and there are shoals and drop-offs. It has baitfish, native fish and fingerlings stocked by helicopter. The wild trout in this pond know how to put on the feed bag. When we catch a brook trout in Munn Pond, we will be counting the pounds not the inches.

There are three times we like to fish Munn Pond. First is right after ice out. The water slowly warms, and the forage fish move into the shallows of the pond. The big brook trout are not far behind. We like to cast sinking lines and big streamers to attract these trout. There is structure that has fallen in the pond, and this makes good targets for casting your streamer. We like to cast the Gray Ghost, Mickey Finn, Light Edson Tiger, Dark Edson Tiger, Muddler and Supervisor. Any of these flies will elicit a strike, so be ready.

The next time we like to fish Munn Pond is after the aerial stocking of fingerlings by New Hampshire Fish and Game. Brook trout are cannibals. If they have their choice, they will feast on their own young. Couple that with

Check tippet often.

the fact that hatchery trout are lost in a natural environment, and the large brook trout go on a feeding frenzy. The Little Brook Trout Bucktail is the only fly you need for this hatch. We again seek out the structure along the shoreline of the pond. Look for fingerling trout to literally be leaping out of the water. This is a sign that a large brook trout is chasing the school of fingerlings and looking for a meal.

The last time that we head to Munn Pond is September. September is the month that brook trout start to get their spawning colors, male brook trout get territorial, the pond water starts to cool off and the fish come out of their summer slumber. Munn Pond in September is a sensory overload—cool waters, fall foliage, brook trout in spawning colors. When you catch one of these big-humped, hook-jawed male brook trout, you will never forget it. The flies we use during the pre-spawn are all bright colors: Chartreuse AD Better Bait Fish, Chartreuse Soft Hackle Streamer, Humungous, Cardinelle and Montreal Whore. The bigger the fly, the bigger the response.

A last word about Munn—this is a big fishpond. That means that you will fish all day and perhaps catch just one fish. It will be the fish of a lifetime.

SESSIONS POND is the last of our brook trout ponds in the Route 16 corridor of the Androscoggin River. It is more than forty acres, making it a nice float tube or canoe pond. Because Sessions Pond is a remote hike-in pond, we prefer to use our float tubes. The redeeming feature of Sessions Pond is the depth. This pond is deeper than most at thirty-four feet, but the average depth is sixteen feet deep. It is ideal for fishing with sinking lines.

As it is a deeper, sinking-line pond, we like to fish six-weight lines here. The heavier line helps to cast the streamers, especially when it gets windy. Since we are casting with a heavier fly line, we will fish streamers in sizes two through six, using Black Nose Dace, Gray Ghost, Black Ghost Marabou, Red Gray Ghost, Supervisor and Light Edson Tiger. These are classic brook trout flies that will deliver the response that we expect from Sessions Pond.

Fish these streamers using the countdown method. This is the best way to determine the level that the fish are found. If fish are marked in shallower water—less than sixteen feet—we fish the east end of the pond. Look for structure and areas where forage is available for the trout. If fish are found deeper than sixteen feet, we like to fish the west end of the pond. This portion of the pond has steeper drop-offs where fish can forage and then return to deeper, cooler water.

Sessions Pond receives a fingerling stocking from New Hampshire Fish and Game in June. This is the time to break out the Little Brook Trout

Woody debris provide good trout habitat.

Bucktail and kick around the pond with your float tube. Look for fingerling trout to break the surface as the larger holdover and native brook trout chase them for a meal.

Dry fly fishing should be fun in Sessions Pond. We have only hit the hatches early in the evening, as we try to get back on the trail before dark. We have had success with the White Wulff, Royal Wulff, Stimulator, Dun Variant, Renegade and Adams. Try to match the size to the natural that is hatching and then match the color. We like to observe trout that are actively feeding and try to anticipate the direction the trout are moving. We will then throw the fly in the direction that we think the trout are traveling and wait for the take. It is a fun way to dry fly fish for these feisty trout.

It can take some time to learn how to locate the fish here. Once the fish are found, you will always remember the spot you "learned."

PHILLIPS BROOK is our favorite brook to fish in the town of Dummer. You access it from Stark off Route 110. Take Paris Road to Phillips Brook Road. We skip the portion of the brook in Stark. We enjoy going out into the woods and exploring the pools and riffles of the brook. Woods roads crisscross the brook. This means that you can park at one bridge, fish upstream or downstream to the next bridge and then take the road back to your car.

There are several beaver flowages that are part of Phillips Brook. Be aware that you can suddenly find one of these gold mines for wild brook trout. Take care when you reach one of these flowages, as the grounds can get swampy quickly. You do not want to get stuck in here and have to wait for someone to get you out. As we approach a beaver flowage, we take a wide berth around the flowage until we reach the dam. We then get out onto the dam and cast to the trout from that position.

When fishing the brook, we use the classic wet flies. Our favorites include the Royal Coachman, Lead Wing Coachman, Campbell's Fancy, Silver Prince, Professor and Wooly Worm. Feed line and let the current take the fly down into the riffle water or the pool. Guide the fly toward structure and strip quickly to illicit a strike.

Fishing from the top of the beaver flowage, we use dry flies, including Royal Wulff, PMX Royal, Yellow Humpy, Elk Hair Caddis, Renegade and Devil Bug. Beaver flowage brook trout are savage, and if there are trout in the flowage, you will know within a few casts. If there is no response, keep moving down the brook.

Bog Brook is our final stop in the Great North Woods. Bog Brook is a tributary to the Androscoggin River. While you can find native brook trout in Bog Brook, we like this one because it leads us to our favorite spot on the Androscoggin River. Using Bog Brook as the entry point to the Androscoggin River, wade out into the river and get the full experience of fishing a *big* river.

The Andro (the local anglers' nickname for the Androscoggin) is a big brawling water that has brook trout, rainbow trout, brown trout and landlock salmon. When we catch all four species in one outing, we have completed an Andro Slam.

The Andro has several safety challenges that the angler should prepare to encounter. The bottom of the river is slick, so we break out the studs and screw them into the bottom of our wading boots. Other anglers choose to wear felt-soled wading boots. Either one will help you stay upright as you lean into the current. We wear inflatable sets of personal floatation devices. This life jacket inflates instantly when you pull the tab. It lays flat against your chest until you need to use it, keeping bulk to a minimum and not interfering with your casting. We are always cautious when fishing anywhere on the Andro—better to be safe than sorry.

A *Zebra caddis*, known locally as the alder fly, hatches from the middle of June until the end of the month. In some years, this hatch is so prolific that there are clouds of bugs as they hatch. The caddis come to rest on the alder bushes that line the river. When we want to know if the hatch is "on," we simply shake an alder branch and watch to see if bugs fly off the bush.

There is a specific alder fly that is stocked in any of the local fly shops in the area. These flies are a specific size and color, and they all have the most redeeming feature, antenna. Cast all of the caddis flies you have, but if they don't have antenna, it's just casting practice.

The alder fly hatch is the last hatch when the angler can catch any of the big fish in the Andro before fall fishing commences. This is Christmas for the anglers who love the Andro. Once word is out that the alder fly hatch is on, all the popular spots off Route 16 fill with anglers. This is why we like Bog Brook.

Bog Brook is on the lesser-traveled east shore of the Andro. We cross the river in Milan and take East Side Road until we are opposite the Pontook Dam. Look for a woods road and follow that road until you reach Bog Brook. After we rig up, we fish the brook until we reach the river. Wade into the river as far as you are comfortable. This is an individual decision, but we always err on the side of caution. The Andro is a dam-controlled river, and flows can change unexpectedly.

Below Bog Brook is a nice piece of flat water that tumbles into some riffle water. If we don't see any alder flies dancing above the water, we shake the alder bushes next to us. This will tell us exactly what type of fishing we are going to have for the evening. Once the hatch starts, fish will begin rising almost instantly. We watch to determine the rise patterns and cast accordingly. A drag-free drift is mandatory. Once the fly has reached the end of the drift, we raise our rod and pull the fly quickly across the surface of the river. This will imitate a skittering alder fly, and fish will strike.

We will fish this hatch until we can no longer see to thread a new fly to our leader. The fishing is that good. Alder flies hatch all along the Andro from Errol to Berlin, so you can do some exploring. However, we just gave you one of the secret waters.

2

WHITE MOUNTAIN NATIONAL FOREST

WILD RIVER WILDERNESS AREA

The **WILD RIVER** is the center of activity in this section of the White Mountain National Forest. It is one of those rivers that has changed quite a bit over the years. Between catastrophic weather events and the introduction of non-native rainbow trout by the State of Maine, the Wild River is a shadow of its former self. In years gone by, we would park at the campground and hike up the Wild River trail to the Spruce Brook tenting area. This would be our base of operations. From this area, we had plenty of feeder brooks and beaver flowages to fish, and the brook trout fishing was nonstop.

Maine began an intensive program of stocking rainbow trout in the Androscoggin River in the 1980s. The rainbow trout began to hold over and inhabit the Wild River. Soon anglers were catching wild rainbow trout in the Wild River. Anglers were intrigued by the new species, which were often wild. The State of New Hampshire received this feedback and started to stock the Wild River with rainbow trout. Now the die was cast. As rainbow trout held over and reproduced, they moved up the Wild River and into the native brook trout habitat. Needless to say, the brook trout, as they do in all Appalachian Mountain streams, are losing the turf war with the rainbow trout.

A second dagger to the native brook trout was Hurricane Irene. This 2011 hurricane destroyed miles and miles of vital trout habitat on the

Plunge pools hold many trout.

Wild River. It will take a very long time for the Wild River to recover from this devastation.

So, why is the Wild River a fly-fishing secret? There are still portions of the Wild River and its tributaries that can give an enjoyable day on the water fly fishing for either brook trout or rainbow trout. The Spruce Brook tent site is at the junction of Spruce Brook and the Wild River. If water is flowing well enough in Spruce Brook, a quick hike up the brook will yield some willing brook trout. The same holds true for the Wild River. If there is enough water flowing, then fish upstream from the tent site. The last time we fished here, it was still all native brook trout.

When we choose to stay overnight at the tent site, we also fish downstream on the Wild River. We fish as far as the junctions with Cedar Brook and Cypress Brook. These brooks add cooler water to the Wild River, but this is also where we caught some wild rainbow trout the last time we fished at this location.

On the second day of our stay, we fish from the junction of Cypress Brook back to the campground. As we fish, we notice a difference in the fish that we are catching. In each pool there will be a change to more rainbow trout and more stocked fish. The stocked fish are a combination of brook trout and

A nice dark brookie from a hemlock forest.

rainbow trout, and they are eager like most stocked trout. Every deep pool holds a couple of fish of either variety.

As the Wild River continues its journey to the Androscoggin River in Maine, don't hesitate to stop along the road and jump into the river to fish the many pools and riffle runs. There are plenty of trout around, and if it has been a warm summer, many large rainbow trout will seek thermal refuge in the cooler waters of the Wild River.

Flies we like for the Wild River drainage fall into two categories: flies for wild fish and flies for hatchery fish. For the wild fish, we like the bushy dry flies like the Royal Wulff, Royal Trude, Royal Stimulator, PMX Royal, White Wulff, Grizzly Wulff, Red Humpy and Yellow Humpy. For stocked fish, we like the Muddler (fished wet and dry), Llama, Elk Hair Caddis, Big Black Stonefly, Golden Stonefly and Mop Flies.

The Wild River holds secret waters—you just need to decide what part of the secret that you want to unfold.

RATTLE RIVER starts at the edge of the Wild River Wilderness and travels northward into the Androscoggin River. As a tributary to the Andro, Rattle is another river that holds both brook trout and rainbow trout. The rainbow trout enter from the Androscoggin River. The cooler waters of the Andro draw the rainbow trout in as a thermal refuge. If the water is too low, the

Loons mean wilderness and trout.

Remote pond flora.

Connecticut Lakes have wild areas.

Covered bridges lead to wild trout.

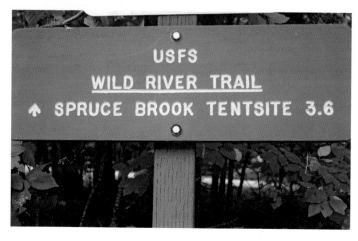

Many hike-in locations allow camping.

Fall means added beauty.

The White Mountains keep waters cool year-round.

Mount Washington is New Hampshire's highest peak.

Trout colors match the stream bottom.

Nesting loons.

Taking a break from the tube.

Sawyer Pond.

Look for junction pools.

Second Connecticut Lake tributary.

Some wild trout do
get parasites.

A nice dark
brookie from a
hemlock forest.

A lake-run fish
from a tributary.

Natural barrier on the Ammonusuc River.

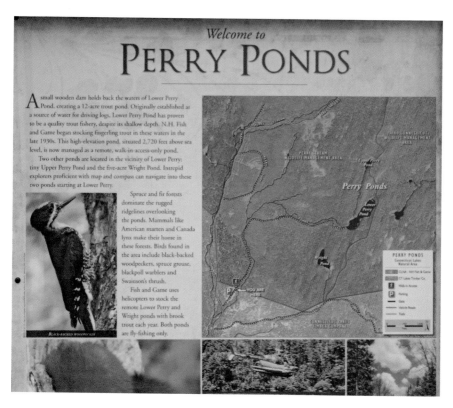

New Hampshire Fish and Game provides information.

Drop a weighted nymph and hold on.

Trout are waiting for your dry fly.

One trout per hole.

Longer rods give you reach.

Wild fungi add beauty.

New Hampshire has many quality trout waters.

Upper Hall Pond in Sandwich.

Fall is a prime time for brook trout.

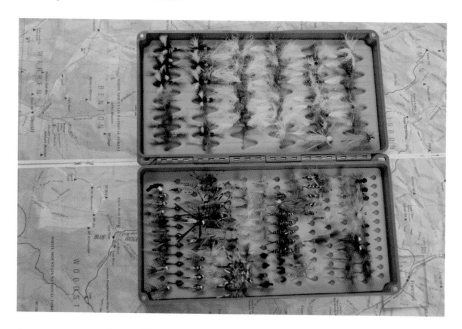

A nice assortment of trout flies.

Left: Some necessary equipment.

Below: Tenkara makes hike-in fishing easy.

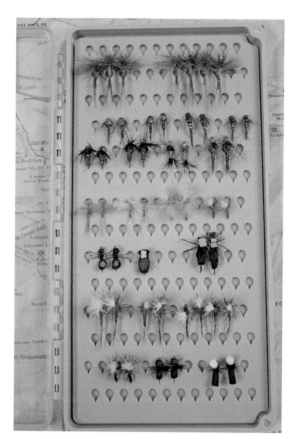

Right: A Saco River assortment.

Below: A wild brook trout assortment.

rainbow trout congregate at the mouth of Rattle River, and there are times when we see more big rainbow trout than anywhere else in New Hampshire.

The Rattle River trail starts at the parking area on Route 2. With the exception of holiday weekends, there is ample parking. It is a little over a mile to the Rattle River shelter and the pool. We have not caught any rainbow trout above this location, but that is always subject to change. When we choose to continue on the trail, we hike another mile and come to a set of cascades. This is about the highest we hike, as we want to have enough time to fish the river back to the parking area.

The Rattle River has some of the same issues as the Wild River. Hurricane Irene was not nice to the Rattle, and the habitat is varied. Many of the plunge pools are void of instream and overhead cover. Look for the deepest pools—trout are good at knowing when they are deep enough that the kingfishers can't spear them and turn them into a meal.

Above the shelter, we like to use our classic wet flies like the Silver Doctor, Orange Fish Hawk, Brown Hackle, Gray Hackle, Royal Coachman and Wooly Worm. For dry flies we use the Bivisible, Dun Variant, Grizzly Wulff, Yellow Humpy, Doodle Bug and Ausable Wulff. The wild brook trout attack these flies with reckless abandon. We float these flies through a pool or riffle

Basin Pond and Evans Notch.

run, and if we don't illicit a strike, we keep moving downstream to the next pool. We cover as much water as we can.

Starting at the pool, we change tactics. You will begin to catch rainbow trout after this spot in the river. We switch to tight-line nymph fishing. This method uses heavy nymphs with a soft hackle as a dropper or positioned off your tippet ring. We always use a Mop fly in chartreuse, yellow or pink as our anchor fly. For the soft hackle we use Hare's Ear, Pheasant Tail, Partridge and Yellow, Sparkle Emerger, Spider and Caddis Emerger.

Drop this rig into every piece of pocket water, no matter how small. We have been amazed at the rainbow trout we have caught in water that wasn't twelve inches wide. This is why we need to fish a tight-line nymph rig in this section of the river.

During terrestrial season, we fish at the mouth of the Rattle River. Throw big hopper patterns, cricket patterns or ant patterns. The rainbow trout go crazy for these flies, and terrestrial fishing extends the season during the month of August. Patterns we like are Moodah Poodah, Transfoamer, Big Eye Hopper, Blingnobyl Ant, Drop Arse Ant and Letort Cricket.

We would like to hike to the Rattle River shelter and stay the night; unfortunately, the Rattle River trail is part of the Appalachian Trail, so the shelter seems to be occupied every time we hike-in to fish.

BASIN POND is a quiet, little body of water on the eastern edge of the Wild River Wilderness. It is part of a Forest Service campground, and we hardly ever see any anglers on the pond. We stumbled on this hidden jewel several years ago while on a family camping trip. We never pass the opportunity to fish this pond when we are in this neck of the woods.

Basin Pond is an artificially created pond. It is not very deep and measures about forty acres. While this pond can be fished with a float tube, we prefer to use a canoe. There is a cartop boat launch. The setting is beautiful, and we are just as happy to paddle around the pond and take in the splendor of Mother Nature. The fishing is a bonus.

This pond is stocked annually by New Hampshire Fish and Game with standard hatchery brook trout. These trout do not seem to last very long in Basin Pond. When we fish Basin Pond later in the season, we catch only wild brook trout.

There are two places to focus on when fishing Basin Pond. The first is the outlet end of the pond. This is the deepest section of the pond and stays coldest longest. We fish streamers here with a sink-tip line, using Woolly Bugger, Black Nose Dace, Little Brook Trout Bucktail and Light Edson Tiger.

It appears that the hatchery trout mostly stay in this bowl in the pond. You will alternate between catching hatchery brook trout and dace, especially in the summer when the pond heats up.

We found the second place by accident. We were doing a leisurely paddle around the pond waiting for the moose to enter the water. Halfway up the southern shore we caught a nice wild brook trout on a Hornberg we were trolling behind the canoe. We made a circle out into the middle of the pond and caught another brook trout. We paddled back over to the original spot and caught another brook trout. This continued for about an hour. It was too much fun.

When releasing the brook trout, the water was noticeably cooler than the rest of the pond. We can only surmise that we found a spring hole or two at this part of Basin Pond. It was a gift that kept on giving.

There is dry fly fishing on Basin Pond. Depending on the time of year, we fish Royal Wulff, White Wulff, PMX Royal, Black Ant, Elk Hair Caddis and Quill Gordon. The downside to the dry fly fishing is that half the time you will catch a dace instead of a trout. We do most of our dry fly fishing on Basin Pond before the Fourth of July. This keeps the dace catch to a minimum.

GREAT GULF WILDERNESS AREA

The **PEABODY RIVER** begins in the Great Gulf Wilderness and ends at the Androscoggin River in Gorham. There is not a more rugged, more beautiful, more misunderstood watershed in the state of New Hampshire. The Peabody River was the poster child for wild brook trout in New Hampshire. In the 1970s, you could stop anywhere along the river and catch brook trout. Like all brook trout rivers in New Hampshire, the farther upstream you hiked, the wilder the brook trout. It was just a fantastic wild brook trout stream.

Once the rainbow trout took hold in the Androscoggin River, these trout began to migrate up into the Peabody River. The intrusion was minimal at first. The rainbow trout stayed in the lower stretches of the river. Soon, New Hampshire Fish and Game began to stock rainbow trout directly into the Peabody River. This began the downfall of the native brook trout.

Brook trout used to be plentiful at the Dolly Copp Picnic area. The last time we fished that section of the Peabody all we caught were rainbow trout—many of them small wild parr. We moved upriver to the Great Gulf trailhead. This water went back to native brook trout. As of the summer of 2018, this section of the river now holds wild rainbow trout. It has also received a stocking of rainbow trout. New Hampshire Fish and Game continues to add to the decline of this once great brook trout fishery.

We continue to hike up the Great Gulf Trail in pursuit of the once great brook trout. These survivors are holding on with everything they have. The Long Island Rapids may be their Alamo. If rainbow trout get past the rapids, then the wild brook trout of the Peabody will be lost. Heaven forbid!

We have a passion for the Peabody River and its great brook trout habitat. We could fish there every week during the summer and never lose our wonder for this great river and the wilderness in which it lives. As we hike up the Great Gulf trail, the smells and the sounds take you back to a time we only dream about. To drop down into the river, cast a Royal Coachman wet fly, feel the tug of a brook trout and hold that jewel in your hand—there is nothing else in the world like it.

Until there is a suspension of the stocking of invasive trout in the Peabody River, we are not going to divulge specific locations for you to visit. We are going to ask that you do your own exploration and make your own memories. Then we are going to ask that you let New Hampshire Fish and Game know that you want them to help save this river from destruction.

We will, however, tell you the flies and techniques we use. After all, we want you to hold these jewels in your hands and understand just how precious native brook trout are. We fish three-weight rods in longer length in the Peabody River. We like to fish dry flies upstream and then wet flies and nymphs on our return trip. Dry flies we like are PMX Royal, White Wulff, Royal Trude, Lime Humpy, Doodle Bug and Stimulator. We cast these to the heads of the pools with a slack line cast and watch the fly on a drag-free drift. The currents are tricky. Once we lose our drag-free drift, we pick up our fly and cast again. We tend to use bigger dry flies, sizes ten to fourteen, so the flies are too big to hook the smaller parr (three inches or smaller).

On our way back downstream, we tight line nymph. We use the Mop Fly as our anchor fly and either a Prince nymph or a Zug Bug nymph as the dropper. The pools on the Peabody can be several feet deep, so you will need to have your tight line technique perfected to catch trout on your return trip down the river.

The Peabody River is a fantastic secret water. We need to make it more popular so that the river can be saved.

Presidential Range—Dry River Wilderness

Rocky Branch starts on the slopes of Mount Isolation and travels down the mountains, ending as a tributary to the Saco River in Glen. This is our first stop for the wonderful wild brook trout fishing that the White Mountains have to offer. There are several ways to fish Rocky Branch, and we will share a couple of our favorites with you.

Our first trip takes us to the Rocky Branch trailhead off of Route 16, six miles north of the town of Jackson. We park at the trailhead and hike the three miles to the Rocky Branch no. 2 tent site. This tent site was a lean-to site previously. Lean-to sites are being dismantled in many of the wilderness areas in the National Forest. It is good that the Forest Service has decided to turn these into tent sites. Check with the Forest Service if you plan to camp at the tent site, as rules do change concerning reservations and numbers of people who can occupy the site.

Once we reach the tent site, we fish Rocky Branch downstream for about two miles or until we reach the trail stream crossings. Because you are in the wilderness portion of the trail, there are no bridges, and crossing the brook, especially in high water, can be dangerous. The brook is skinny this high up, and the fishing is limited to spring and early summer flows. Once

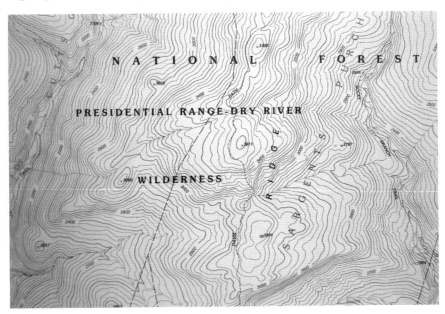

The Dry River Wilderness.

A Rocky Branch brook trout.

the water starts to drop, the fish will move downstream to the bigger water and the deep pools. Early in the season, we fish wet flies and nymphs in this section of Rocky Branch. Wet flies to use are the Professor, Montreal, Brown Hackle, Gray Hackle, Wooly Worm and Mop Fly. Nymphs include the Hare's Ear, Pheasant Tail, Prince, Gray Squirrel, Fullback and Halfback. The nymphs should be weighted or bead head to reach the bottom of the pools on Rocky Branch.

Rocky Branch then leaves the wilderness portion of the national forest and continues through the regular portion. We drive up the Rocky Branch Road from Glen to the southern trailhead. There is ample parking here but not as much as at the northern trailhead. We quickly cross Rocky Branch and follow the trail to Rocky Branch shelter no. 1. This is a lean-to and may stay in place. We fish from the shelter back to the parking area. The trout are wild and beautiful and plentiful. We have never had a bad day fishing this stretch of the brook, until the fall when the trout go on their search for spawning grounds. We often wonder where all the trout we caught in the spring and the summer disappeared to, but do not worry. They are off building next year's class of trout.

We use the same flies in this stretch of Rocky Branch as we use in the upper stretch. Either of these trips give us that wilderness setting, and the number of trout we see is amazing. We have been in love with this brook since we were children and we hope that you will enjoy Rocky Branch as much as we have over the years.

DRY RIVER is the namesake for this wilderness section of the national forest, which is as rugged as any portion of the forest. When we choose to hike the Dry River trail, we take wilderness gear in a pack or rucksack. This is not a leisurely hike. The farther we go upriver, the more potential there is for weather-related events to challenge us. Dry River got its name from the fact that the river is only visible during high-water events. In the summer, we think that the river has gone dry in certain sections. In fact, due to the river bottom substrate, the river continues to run underground. What this means is that any rainstorm that may break out, including quick thunderstorms, can raise the river quickly and leave us stranded until it subsides. Please be careful and plan accordingly.

We begin at the Dry River trailhead at Route 302 in Crawford Notch. Other than the busiest of weekends, you will find parking. The trail travels for about half a mile before you reach the river. It then follows the river with several crossings along the way. Depending on how much time we wish to spend hiking and fishing that day, we can hike the six miles to the Dry River shelter. We stop here to recharge and then start fishing our way back down the river. We keep an eye on time because we can easily get engrossed in catching the wild brook trout and forget how far we are up into the wilderness. This has happened to us on several occasions and resulted in us having to hustle down the trail in near darkness.

A more relaxed way to fish the Dry River is to hike to the Mount Clinton Brook trail intersection and fish down from that point. This is the midpoint of the fishable part of the Dry River, and the Mount Clinton Brook infuses some cold water into the Dry River at this point. Wherever we choose to start our fishing adventure, we make time to stop at one of the big pools and take in the wilderness around us. It is a memory we never forget.

Flies to use on the Dry River include these wet flies: Royal Coachman, Professor, Montreal, Parmachenee Belle, "88" and Wooly Worm. Weighted nymphs include Hare's Ear, Flashback Hare's Ear, Pheasant Tail, Copper, Copper John and Prince. Dry flies include Royal Wulff, White Wulff, Grizzly Wulff, Orange Stimulator, Royal PMX and Black Ant.

Fishing the Dry River involves a time commitment in both planning and execution. Make sure to allow enough time to fully take in the opportunities that the valley of the Dry River has to offer. We think you will be glad you chose this as one of your secret waters.

PEMIGEWASSET WILDERNESS AREA

ETHAN POND is our second of only three ponds in New Hampshire that is classified as a wild trout pond. This pond receives no supplemental stocking, and the brook trout are all native. If you have ever dreamt of fishing for wild brook trout in an isolated pond, this is the place to do it. This pond is a three-mile hike from the Willey House in Crawford Notch. We take the Kedron Falls trail to the Ethan Pond trail. There is a shelter at the pond, and sometimes we elect to spend the night—the fishing is that good. By staying at the Ethan Pond shelter, you also have access to Shoal Pond—the other wild trout pond in the wilderness.

We hike our float tubes into Ethan Pond. The pond is only four acres and four feet deep. It is spring fed, which keeps the waters cool in the summer and keeps the pond from freezing solid in the winter. We bring a nine-foot, four-weight fly rod into Ethan Pond with a floating line. Because the pond is shallower, we can fish with weighted flies if we feel the need to fish the bottom of the pond. When we do want to fish the bottom of the pond, we use the Harris Special, Wooly Worm or Hornberg.

The remainder of the time, we fish wet flies and dry flies. Wet flies we like include Royal Coachman, White Miller, March Brown, Light Cahill, "88" and Professor. For dry flies, we like White Wulff, PMX Royal, Yellow Humpy, Dun Variant, Balloon Caddis and Adams. When the trout are feeding, any of these flies will bring nonstop action. If we get to Ethan Pond in the early afternoon, we start fishing with our wet flies. We will

The Pemigewasset Wilderness.

Tent platforms mean you can stay overnight.

let them sink a foot or more and then strip them back. As the sun creeps behind the mountains, we will switch to dry flies and try to take advantage of rising trout. We will continue this until the action stops, usually before total darkness as the pond surface cools off.

While Ethan Pond is small enough to cover the whole pond in our float tube, we tend to focus on the inlet at the east end of the pond and float from there down the north shore where there is another feeder stream. We then focus on the middle of the pond, which holds the deepest water.

Three miles farther west is **SHOAL POND**. Shoal Pond is the third designated wild trout pond in New Hampshire. Shoal has a lot of the same features as Ethan Pond. Shoal Pond is four acres and four feet deep in places. It has inlet streams, one outlet stream and a self-sustaining population of native brook trout.

If you stay at the Ethan Pond shelter, hike to Shoal Pond at daybreak. By the time you reach Shoal Pond, the surface water will be warming, and bug life will be rejuvenated from the nighttime chill. We use the same equipment and flies in Shoal Pond as we used in Ethan Pond. We have found no major difference in what the brook trout will strike.

The pond is small, and we tend to fish all day when we are staying at Ethan Pond shelter. We have found fish all over Shoal Pond, but we tend to gravitate to the north end of the pond where the feeder streams enter the water. We then kick down pond and spend considerable time fishing the southwest corner. The deepest water is located here.

The nice thing about staying at Ethan Pond shelter is that we can stay and fish Shoal Pond until darkness. It is not a bad hike back to Ethan Pond in the twilight, so bring your headlamp.

Another fun pond to fish in the Pemigewasset Wilderness is **BLACK POND**. In fact, we enjoy fishing this entire section of the wilderness. We hike up the Lincoln Woods trail and camp at the Franconia Brook tent site. This becomes our base of operations to enjoy the fishing opportunities in this section of the Pemigewasset Wilderness. Black Pond is a short hike from the tent site. You may need to ford the river from the tent site. Use caution, especially if there is high water. We take the Black Pond trail up to the pond. Black Pond is less than three acres in size, but it is thirty-four feet deep. This depth means only one thing—the potential for some larger-than-average brook trout. Using a float tube allows us to access more of the water than the spin casters and bait anglers who fish from the shore.

Black Pond means sinking lines and streamers. We like to get deep where the bigger brook trout reside. We use bigger hook sizes to keep the smaller trout off our line. Size four and size six are best in Black Pond. Streamers include Light Edson Tiger, Black Ghost, Soft Hackle Streamer, Gray Ghost, Supervisor and Harris Special. We use the Little Brook Trout Bucktail after the New Hampshire Fish and Game aerial stocking.

We need to use the countdown method here and fish the clock. Fish can be found anywhere, so we need to work the entire pond. We start after we kick out of the south end of the pond and get to where the water drops off, and then we work up the west shore to the inlet stream. The pond bottom drops off here, so we work the drop-off thoroughly. Once we find the depth the fish are feeding, we fish it hard. We are typically rewarded.

Because of the difficulty in accessing the tent site, we haven't fished Black Pond in the evening. If you don't mind hiking out three miles in the dark, give it a try. Then it will be your secret water.

FRANCONIA BROOK is great to fish for wild brook trout. We hike up the Franconia Brook trail to the intersection with Hellgate Brook, and then we fish down from that point. You will have a combination of pools, beaver flowages and riffle water. This means that trout are plentiful, and if the beaver flowage is fairly new, brook trout will be on the larger size.

The brook is one of the prettiest in the wilderness. We enjoy the hike up and the fishing back down. We catch so many trout that we take time to stop and enjoy the surroundings. To experience the true wilderness, take the Lincoln Brook trail to where it crosses Franconia Brook and fish down to Franconia Falls from that point. This is more than a mile of bushwhacking fishing, and we never see another footprint.

Because we fish Franconia Brook downstream, we fish wet flies, including Royal Coachman, Professor, Montreal, White Miller, Wooly Worm and Orange Fish Hawk. Let the current take the fly down to a likely holding spot and then strip back. You will get a strike almost immediately. If you don't get a strike after two or three passes of the water, keep moving. A mile of stream doesn't seem like much, but this stretch will take you all day to fish correctly.

In the bigger pools and beaver flowages, use a bushy dry fly—Royal Wulff, White Wulff, PMX Royal, Yellow Stimulator, Elk Hair Caddis and Yellow Humpy. We put on a longer leader to fish these flies. In some of the beaver flowages, the trout will almost knock each other out trying to grab the fly. It is hysterical to watch.

Many anglers fish the east branch of the Pemigewasset River. The farther upstream you hike, the less fishing pressure. The secret water is the **NORTH FORK**, located in the middle of the wilderness. We have never seen another angler fishing this tributary of the Pemigewasset. There is no quick way to reach this wild brook trout water.

We approach it from the south following the Pemi East Side trail. We are often tempted to stop and fish the East Branch of the Pemigewasset along the way, but it is such a long hike that we can not delay. When we reach the Thoreau Falls trail, we put the hike into overdrive. If we don't, we end up fishing the East Branch when we reach the crossing. Time will not be on our side.

After about a mile on the Thoreau Falls trail, we can see the North Fork. We drop down into the brook and fish back down to the junction with the east branch. Depending on time, we will fish downstream on the East Branch until we see the trail. By that time, we know we will have to get moving if we want a spot at the Franconia Brook tent site.

North Fork is a small wild brook trout water. We always go with barbless hooks when we fish here. Wet flies and soft hackles are the go-to flies here—Brown Hackle, Gray Hackle, Sparkle Emerger, Black Spider, Partridge and Yellow and White Miller. There are a few locations to fish dry flies. Bushy, high-floating flies include Royal Wulff, Grizzly Wulff and White Wulff. We rarely have time to switch leaders and throw dry flies, but perhaps you will.

SANDWICH RANGE WILDERNESS AREA

GUINEA POND is a fantastic little brook trout pond found just outside the Sandwich Range Wilderness. This is the first of several ponds that we are drawn to fish whenever we are in the area. Guinea Pond is relatively easy to reach. It is a two-mile hike along an abandoned railroad bed, which makes for easy walking while carrying your float tube. Guinea Pond is about eleven acres, and the pond has a deep spot in the northeast corner that is more than twenty feet deep. It is the ideal float tube pond.

There is a sign that points to the spur off the Guinea Pond trail to lead to the pond. We rig up our nine-foot, four-weight rod with a sink-tip line, hop in the float tube and start fishing. Flies we start with include Black Ghost, Humungous, Muddler Minnow, Wooly Bugger, Mickey Finn and Maynard Marvel. These flies are good locators for Guinea Pond. Use the countdown method to find the depth the fish are feeding. Ice goes out later in Guinea Pond, so if you get there early in the season, this is a winning strategy. Guinea Pond receives a fingerling stocking from New Hampshire Fish and Game.

As the waters warm, we switch to fishing with our floating lines and emerger patterns, such as Sparkle Soft Hackle, CJ Controller, Catchall Spider, Emerger Caddis, Low Hanging Fruit and Bi Focal Emerger. There is

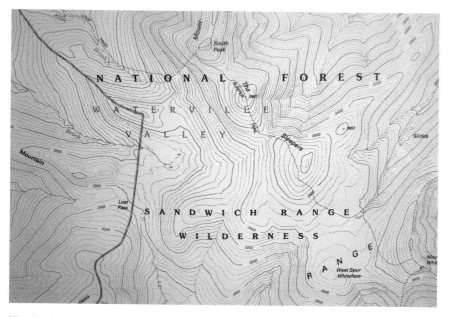

The Sandwich Range Wilderness.

plenty of insect activity in Guinea Pond, so we like to prospect with emerger patterns until we find a size or color on which the brook trout focus. If emergers are not drawing a response, we will use the Hornberg, Yellow Hornberg or Yellow Wooly Worm.

Hatch activity at dusk can be wild. We have been to Guinea Pond when it looks like it is raining, with fish rising all over the pond. Most nights it is more typical. We have had luck with many of the Catskill dry flies—Pink Lady, Quill Gordon, Hendrickson, Light Cahill, Adams and Beaverkill. For modern dry flies, we like the Klinkhammer and the Kicking Klinkhammer. Match the size and then the color of the bugs that are hatching.

On our way to Guinea Pond, we pass the trail to **Black Mountain Pond**. Black Mountain Pond is the headwater of the Beebe River. The pond is a little bigger than six acres. The average depth is ten feet, but Black Mountain Pond has that large brook trout hole that goes more than thirty feet deep.

Once you start up the Black Mountain Pond trail, you cross into the Sandwich Range Wilderness. The trail follows the Beebe River. Don't get distracted by the good-looking water or any of the beaver flowages that may have formed. Concentrate on the task at hand.

After hiking the two and a half miles, put your sink-tip line on your nine-foot, four-weight outfit. This is a three-line pond. You will be using your sinking line and your floating line on the pond. Where you enter the pond with your float tube is the shallower part of the pond. We start with some of our basic wet fly patterns, Professor, Hornberg, Yellow Hornberg, Royal Coachman, Brown Hackle and Gray Hackle. Cast flies toward any structure that can be seen through the clear water. We typically catch smaller trout in this area.

As you kick across the pond, the water drops off and then rises up again. We change to our sinking line because we are now fishing deeper water. This means streamers, including Soft Hackle, Muddler, Black Ghost, Humungous, Harris Special and Maynard Marvel. Use the countdown method and fish the clock. Continue over the shallower water until you see the bottom drop off again. You are now casting into the deepest part of the pond. If there are any larger fish, they will be here. Be ready. Black Mountain Pond is aerial stocked in June by New Hampshire Fish and Game, so don't forget your Little Brook Trout Bucktail.

As it is in a wilderness area, there is no shelter at Black Mountain Pond. This makes the decision to stay and fish the evening hatch difficult. In wet summer, there are stream crossings that should not be attempted in the dark. For this reason, we have never stayed to fish this hatch. When we decide to attempt fishing the evening hatch in dry times, the dry fly fishing can be great. Dry flies we would try include Royal Wulff, White Wulff, Grizzly Wulff, PMX Royal, Orange Stimulator and Elk Hair Caddis. It could be a memorable night.

A quick note: when planning to spend several days in this area, don't forget to fish the Beebe River. This section of the Beebe River is wild brook trout water. When we want to have some fast action, or we were skunked on Black Mountain Pond, the Beebe River can save the day. Use the same wet flies that you used in Black Mountain Pond.

If we want to rest our legs for a day, we head to **UPPER HALL POND.** Upper Hall Pond is just outside the wilderness but is still in the National Forest. It is part of a trio of ponds that all hold wild brook trout. We drive to Upper Hall Pond, and it has a cartop boat launch, though no motors are allowed on the water. Upper Hall Pond is forty-eight acres, and most of it runs deep. When we bring a canoe, we can cover most of the pond. We will troll a streamer trying to locate trout. Once we get to the outlet end of the pond, we will anchor and fish the rocky portions around the island. Due to fishing pressure and loon predation, Upper Hall Pond is stocked by New Hampshire Fish and Game. There is also natural reproduction of brook trout here.

This is a three-line pond. We typically start with our sink-tip line and streamers. Streamers we like include Black Ghost, Gray Ghost, Supervisor, Mickey Finn, Harris Special and Maynard Marvel. We troll these around the pond until we get a strike. We then anchor the canoe and fish the clock using the countdown method. This is very successful at Upper Hall Pond.

Dry fly action is also very good at Upper Hall Pond. We like to try to match the hatch here, using Quill Gordon, Hendrickson, Klinkhammer, Kicking Klinkhammer, March Brown and Griffiths Gnat. Being able to get in and out of Upper Hall Pond lets us fish until we can't see to tie on a new fly. And we do.

When all else fails, we put on a full-sink line and dredge the depths of Upper Hall Pond. The pond drops off quickly from the bump out on the western shore. We lazily float along this portion of the pond waiting for our flies to reach the depths. We have had success using two different fly strategies: large nymphs and small steamers. For nymphs, we like Hare's Ear, Golden Stone, Black Stone, Halfback and Montana. For streamers, we use Harris Special, Hornberg, Yellow Hornberg and Maynard Marvel. This fishing is slower but can be very rewarding. We have caught brook trout more than sixteen inches using this method.

MIDDLE HALL POND is all about the sinking lines. This pond is less than ten acres and more than forty feet deep. It is the definition of a kettle pond. Using the countdown method from our float tube, we can cover this pond easily. Early in the season the fish are in shallow waters, but it doesn't take long for the waters to warm and the fish to gravitate to cooler, deeper waters. When we visit Middle Hall Pond, we bring a streamer box with the following streamers: Black Ghost, Gray Ghost, Complex Twist Bugger, Sculpin Snack, Harris Special and Hornberg. We put these flies in different hook sizes from four through ten. If the fish are eating, we are catching once we have the depth and hook size dialed in. If we fish this pond after the aerial stocking by New Hampshire Fish and Game, we use the Little Brook Trout Bucktail in size six or size eight.

LOWER HALL POND is exactly the opposite of Middle Hall Pond. It is long and shallow. We like to fish this pond with our floating fly line and long leaders. For wet flies, we like Professor, Montreal, Silver Prince, Trout Fin, Parmachenee Belle and Leisenring's Tups. For emergers, we like Brown Hackle, Gray Hackle, Sparkle Emerger, Fripple, Low Hanging Fruit and Partridge and Yellow. For nymphs, we like Hare's Ear, Pheasant Tail, Wooly Worm, Rainbow Warrior, Zug Bug and Tellico. New Hampshire Fish and

Great way to spend a summer day.

Game stocks more than three thousand fingerlings in this pond. We have always caught endless small trout here—to the point of silliness. We have not caught any larger trout. That might be because we left the Little Brook Trout Bucktail at home.

Middle Hall Pond can be reached by following the trail from Upper Hall Pond. Lower Hall Pond can be reached by a trail off Lower Hall Pond Road—a very rough road off Algonquin Road. Float tubes are mandatory.

FLAT MOUNTAIN POND is a beautiful twenty-eight-acre pond that is loaded with brook trout and is managed by New Hampshire Fish and Game as a remote trout water. Flat Mountain Pond is a five-mile hike over mostly smooth trail with an elevation climb of approximately fifteen hundred feet. The trail begins at Whiteface Intervale Road. This is a long, narrow pond running northeast to southwest, so winds can be a factor when float tubing the pond. If the wind is out of the southwest, we hike the extra mile to the southern end of the pond, so we can have some help floating to the north end. We will do this if we are planning to stay overnight, so we can claim the Flat Mountain Pond shelter.

When we start at the southern end, we are immediately in small native brook trout. These fish will attack your fly. We use our nine-foot, four-weight rod. Because it takes us three hours to reach the pond, when starting at the southern end, we use our floating line and dry flies. Favorite dry flies are Elk Hair Caddis, Royal Wulff, White Wulff, Doodle Bug, Bivisible and Yellow Stimulator.

As you kick down the pond, the water will gradually get deeper. This is where the larger trout in the pond seek refuge. We switch to our sink-tip lines and longer leaders. Try using a Harris Special, Maynard Marvel, Wardens Worry, Light Edson Tiger, Hornberg or Soft Hackle Streamer. Use the countdown method and fish the clock to find fish in the water column. You never know when the big one will strike (big being ten and twelve inches). Flat Mountain Pond receives an annual aerial stocking from Fish and Game. When fishing around that time, don't forget the Little Brook Trout Bucktail. Fish the inlet, as this is the deepest part of Flat Mountain Pond.

Due to the elevation, temperature in the pond stays fairly cool throughout the season, so it is a rare day that we will go fishless. If that does seem to be the case, we soak in the beauty of this pond. Many times, one of the resident beavers will greet us with a tail slap.

ALGONQUIN BROOK is our favorite moving water spot in this area of the Sandwich Range Wilderness. We access this brook from Sandwich Notch Road. There is a small pull-off right at the bridge crossing. We hike up the Algonquin trail to where it crosses the brook. This is small-stream fishing. We use our short rod, three-weight setup to fish here. The wild brook trout go crazy for wet flies or nymphs. Wet flies include Royal Coachman, Professor, Brown Hackle, Gray Hackle, Orange Fish Hawk and Pink Lady. We only use one nymph here, the Mop Fly. Colors that drive the wild brook trout crazy include yellow, orange, chartreuse, pink, cream and brown.

We fish downstream under the bridge until we reach the confluence with the outlet to Lower Hall Pond. The trout here are that dark black that is just gorgeous. Be careful wading this brook, as the rocks do tend to be slippery. But fishing here for wild brook trout is totally worth the effort.

OTHER WHITE MOUNTAIN NATIONAL FOREST SECRET WATERS

In the northern-most reaches of the White Mountain National Forest are several mountain streams that contain native brook trout. You can choose any of the thin blue lines in Stark, Kilkenny or Berlin and have a memorable day with these fish. Our favorite way to cover this territory is to take York Pond Road to Bog Dam Road and do the loop. This loop crosses many brooks, and all of them have wild brook trout.

This area is the headwaters to the Upper Ammonoosuc River. The brooks are beautiful trout water, and we just like to drive along Bog Dam Road and choose whichever brook looks to have a good flow of water. We try to get to these streams when the leaves on the alder bushes are the size of a mouse's ear. This means that the waters are warming, the bugs are getting active and the trout are feeding.

REFUGE BROOK, STONY BROOK AND BEND BROOK are good places to try. If you want a wilderness experience, take the Upper Ammonoosuc trail. It dissects the loop you are driving, and the farther away you get from the road, the better the fishing.

We like to fish classic wet flies for these native brook trout, including Royal Coachman, Silver Prince, Queen of Waters, Orange Fish Hawk, Wickham's Fancy and Leisenring's Gray Hackle. For dry flies, we like Royal Wulff, White

Natural barrier on the Ammonoosuc River.

Wulff, Bivisible, Elk Hair Caddis, Parachute Adams and Klinkhammer. If you don't catch fish on these flies, then the fish are not biting that day.

York Pond Road is off Route 110 in Berlin. It is the road to New Hampshire Fish and Game's Barry Camp, which is used to teach fishing and hunting to the next generation of anglers and hunters. The roads are usually in decent condition, and you should have no problems traveling and searching for your next wild brook trout adventure.

JEFFERSON BROOK starts on Mount Jefferson and travels down the mountain until it reaches the Ammonoosuc River just below Cog Railway Base Road. Jefferson Brook is your prototypical native brook trout stream in the White Mountains. We like to start fishing Jefferson Brook after we have hiked or biked the two miles from where Jefferson Notch Road leaves Cog Base Road. Jefferson Notch Road takes a sharp left and leaves the brook, and this is where we start. The brook is still small at this point, and we fish with our short, three-weight rods and wet flies.

Wet flies we use include the Royal Coachman, Brown Hackle, Gray Hackle, Silver Prince, Campbell's Fancy and Montreal. These flies will bring a willing response if the trout are present. Remember to keep moving down the stream until you find fish. These trout are willing, so fishing a pool longer than three or four minutes is just wasting valuable time.

As you get downstream, the brook widens a little, which makes it dry fly water. Big bushy dries are the best because they stay buoyant and draw vicious strikes from the brook trout. Some of the bigger pools will have trophy (ten-inch) brook trout. These trout will put a big bend in your three-weight rod and give you a memory you won't soon forget. Bushy dry flies we like are the Royal Wulff, White Wulff, Grizzly Wulff, PMX Royal, Yellow Humpy and Lime Trude.

National Forest trails lead to secret waters.

Because Jefferson Brook is so close to the Cog Railway, anglers don't consider fishing here. This is why the angling is so good—there is very little pressure. Most anglers fish the Ammonoosuc River and ignore all the feeder streams into the Ammonoosuc. We have found that several of the feeder streams provide memorable angling for wild brook trout. Just don't tell anyone your secret water.

The **Carter Lakes** take work to hike-in, but the rewards are well worth the effort. There are two ways to hike into these lakes. The most popular, and the one used by day hikers, is the Nineteen Mile Brook trail off Route 16. Because of the popularity, parking can be challenging. Weekdays are the best time to do this hike. The other approach is the Wildcat River trail from the end of Carter Notch Road. You will hike over so much fishable water that you will want to stay over at the Carter Notch Hut.

The Carter Notch Hut is an Appalachian Mountain Club facility. There are approximately forty sleeping locations, and the hut is a stone's throw from the Carter Lakes. During certain times of year, the Appalachian Mountain Club provides meals at the hut. Check in with the AMC in Pinkham Notch for details and pricing for overnight stays and meals. If you can get a bunk, we highly recommend it.

The Carter Lakes provide some exciting fishing for the native brook trout. While you will not catch any trophy trout in these lakes, the setting is simply breathtaking. The Carter Lakes can be iced in until Memorial Day, depending on the condition of the previous winter. We fish these lakes in the middle of the summer, as it has always been cooler at this elevation, and the lake water temperatures are always trout friendly.

For us, these have always been dry fly lakes. The wild trout are aggressive, and we like to cast classic dry flies at these fish. Try the Adams, Quill

Deep dark trout water.

Gordon, Doodle Bug, Royal Coachman, Light Cahill and Griffith's Gnat. If the fish are feeding, they are not very particular. Because we hike in to the Carter Lakes, we bring our shorter three weight rods. These rods don't take much pack space, and due to the length of the trip, we like to have plenty of food and water with us. We also use a small fly box and choose our patterns ahead of time. Whichever flies you choose, bring them in multiple hook sizes. We find it more productive if we can match the size of the hatch.

The weather can change quickly in Carter Notch. Rain and winds can arrive at any time. For this reason, we also bring a few wet flies to throw if it rains. Wet flies we like are the Black Wooly Worm, Yellow Wooly Worm, Brown Hackle, Gray Hackle and Orange Fish Hawk. Let these flies sink below the surface and then do a slow retrieve. You will chuckle at how aggressive the trout can be.

If you choose the Nineteen Mile Brook trail, there may be fish in the brook. We are usually so focused on getting to the Carter Lakes that we have not fished the brook. If you have the time and the inclination, give Nineteen Mile Brook a try.

WILDCAT RIVER is the most productive wild brook trout river in New Hampshire. Starting at the junction with the Ellis River in Jackson all the way to the headwaters in Beans Purchase, no river in New Hampshire packs more wild trout. We can't even begin to count the number of times that the Wildcat River has saved our fishing trip. We absolutely love fishing the Wildcat River.

Two things keep the Wildcat River spectacular. The lower reaches are mostly on private lands, which makes access challenging. The lower reaches have fewer but bigger trout, and the hatches are fantastic. There is something about standing in the middle of the Wildcat River, sun setting behind the mountains, light cahill hatch coming off the water, native brook trout rising. We could dry fly fish in this scenario for the remainder of our lives and never complain.

The upper reaches of the Wildcat River are a hike-in. This keeps fishing pressure to a minimum. Drive to the end of Carter Notch Road and start up the trail. There are several places where the trail follows the river. Jump right in the river and start fishing. The trout in this section of the river are only three to four inches, but they are plentiful. We never tire of fishing for these trout. They are feisty and beautiful. We can tell by looking at them that they are a different strain from other wild brook trout streams.

In the lower reaches we like to fish with dry flies exclusively. During the day we like to fish attractor dry flies in sizes twelve through sixteen, using the Royal Wulff, White Wulff, PMX Royal, Lime Humpy, Bivisible and Yellow Stimulator. These fish see more flies, so they are a little more sophisticated. We use nine-foot leaders in this stretch of the Wildcat River. We fish the flies upstream with a drag-free float. As with all wild trout, the strikes will be savage. Be ready at any moment to raise your rod tip and set the hook.

In the upper reaches, we tend to use the classic wet flies, including Montreal, Professor, Silver Prince, Royal Coachman, Brown Hackle and Orange Fish Hawk. These trout see fewer anglers and are less sophisticated. Wet flies—barbless—in sizes fourteen or sixteen work best. When we only want to hook the fish over six inches, we use flies tied in sizes ten or twelve. The smaller fish will splash at the flies but not hook themselves. Leaders can be as short as five feet in this section of the Wildcat River. Since we are diehard dry fly anglers, we always give it a try. Casting room is minimal, and the short riffle water makes for short drag-free floats.

The Wildcat River is no longer stocked above Jackson Falls. Even below the falls most stocked fish drop down into the Ellis River. If wild brook trout are your thing, and you call a twelve-inch fish a trophy, then the Wildcat River is the one place you should fish.

SLIPPERY BROOK is a small stream in the easternmost section of the White Mountain National Forest. Coming down from Eastman Mountain, Slippery Brook is a tributary to the east branch of the Saco River. Slippery Brook is often overlooked as a brook trout fishery as the East Branch is the popular fishery in this section of the national forest.

Most anglers take the left on Town Hall Road and continue to the headwaters of the East Branch. Those who go right along Slippery Brook Road are driving to the parking area for Mountain Pond. Slippery Brook goes mostly unnoticed. Drive to the end of the road to the trailhead. We like to hike as far as we can and then fish back down Slippery Brook.

Slippery Brook falls from its origin on Eastman Mountain at a 2,500-foot elevation to the parking area at 1,600 feet. Dropping 900 feet in four miles means that there is a lot of meandering pocket water to fish in Slippery Brook. There are plenty of plunge pools and riffle waters. Woody debris creates good cover for the wild brook trout here.

Slippery Brook is smaller, so we fish wet flies. Our favorite wet flies for Slippery Brook are the Royal Coachman, Silver Prince, Campbell Fancy, White Miller, Professor and Wooly Worm. We stand at the head of pools

National Forest road crossings hold trout.

and let the current carry the fly to the tail of the pool. If a brook trout has not grabbed the fly on its way down the pool, fish the fly back up the pool with short quick strips. Fish the fly this way two or three times. If we don't have a strike or see a fish, then we move to the next pool. We cover a lot of Slippery Brook and find a lot of trout fishing this way. We have a lot of fun.

Wachipauka Pond is the westernmost pond that we fish in the White Mountain National Forest. The pond is twenty-two acres and reaches a depth of thirty feet. The hike-in to this pond is more than two miles with some steep sections, so we recommend using a float tube. We understand there have been some trail changes as you approach the pond, so keep an eye out for the access trail.

Wachipauka Pond is under the shadow of Webster Slide Mountain in a beautiful setting. We really enjoy fishing the pond even though it takes a big effort to get there. The trail dumps us off at the north end of the pond. We start with our nine-foot, five-weight rod and a sink-tip line. Early in the season, we will use streamers on our sink-tip line, including Mickey Finn, Black Ghost, Harris Special, Maynard Marvel, Light Edson Tiger and Warden's Worry. We will use the countdown method to locate fish. We fish down the western shore, alternating between casting to shore and casting

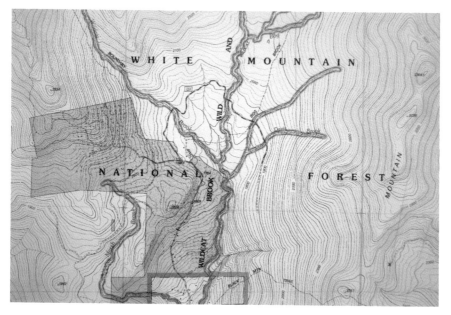

Many headwater streams in the White Mountain National Forest (WMNF).

to the deeper part of the pond. If you go to the pond in June, bring a Little Brook Trout Bucktail. New Hampshire Fish and Game puts fingerlings in the pond at that time.

During the summer, we will fish the same flies on a full sink line. We focus on casting and letting the fly sink deep into the depths of the pond. We call this dredging for trout. It is slow and requires patience but can be well worth the effort. This is just a beautiful place for some concentrated streamer fishing.

In the fall, we tend to gravitate to the outlet areas of the pond. There is natural reproduction in the pond, and we find that the shallow water areas can be productive. This is the time of the year to catch the bigger brook trout. We like to try to get to the pond in the last ten days of September.

Due to the hiking limitations, we have not stayed to fish the pond's evening hatch. We have no reason to not believe that it will be as memorable as our streamer fishing. Since we are not familiar with the hatches, we would recommend trying Royal Wulff, White Wulff, Grizzly Wulff, PMX Royal, Stimulator and Elk Hair Caddis in sizes twelve to sixteen.

The **THREE PONDS** in Warren are an exceptional set of ponds for brook trout fishing. They all have their own character. The hike-in to the ponds is a leisurely two and a half miles, so if one pond isn't producing, we can quickly get to one of the others. If we are at the ponds and fishing is memorable, we can stay at the Three Ponds shelter and make a weekend out of our trip. The float tube is the fishing craft of choice. These ponds are spring fed, so locating the cooler water is imperative to success.

We start at the **UPPER POND**. This pond is twelve acres, and the center is ten feet deep. The average depth is four feet, so we tend to fish with our sink-tip line with our nine-foot, four-weight outfit. We begin with wet flies, including Royal Coachman, Professor, White Miller, Cahill, Hendrickson and "88." We float away from shore and cast back to the structure. We like to start up at the inlet and float diagonally northwest to southeast across the pond. This takes you over the deeper water. Use the countdown method. We will then fish the cove that is the outlet to the pond. This is also the area that we like to dry fly fish. The trout here like the bushy dry flies—Bivisible, Pink Lady Bivisible, Renegade, Royal Wulff, Elk Hair Caddis and PMX Royal. We like sizes fourteen or sixteen.

MIDDLE POND is thirteen acres and runs long and thin. We try to get into the pond at the inlet. The water here is cooler, and there is a deep hole just to the west of the inlet. Brook trout will stack up here. The middle of the pond is the deepest, and we will take our sink-tip line and fish the same wet flies as the Upper Pond. The only addition we would make for Middle Pond is the Yellow Wooly Worm. We find this fly effective in the summer for any springs you locate.

LOWER POND is quirky. It is only three acres and fourteen feet deep. It is a real kettle pond. We have not caught any big brook trout in Lower Pond, but we have caught plenty of brook trout. This pond is a wild brook trout factory. If we don't start catching fish immediately, we get off the pond and go to one of the others.

These ponds are part of the New Hampshire Fish and Game fingerling program. We can always tell the difference between a wild trout and a grown hatchery trout. You will be able to tell the difference as well.

EAST POND is a small wild brook trout pond located in the shadow of Mount Osceola. There are two approaches to the pond, and we like both. The easiest hike is from the Tripoli Road in Waterville Valley. It is a one-and-a-half-mile hike from this southern trailhead. The hike from here is not very steep and can be done while carrying your float tube. East Pond is just over six acres, with a maximum depth of twenty-seven feet. The pond has a population of golden shiners, which makes great forage. We fish using our nine-foot, four-weight outfit with either a floating or a sink-tip line.

Start with a sink-tip line and streamers. We choose from Black Ghost, Mickey Finn, Warden's Worry and Light Edson Tiger. If we are going to fish deeper, we will use the Harris Special or the Maynard Marvel. We also fish the Little Brook Trout Bucktail; however, New Hampshire Fish and Game does not stock this pond.

We float out about thirty feet from shore and cast back toward any structure we see. There are plenty of small trout—and shiners—that will take your fly. When we find this bothersome, we use larger streamers in sizes six or four. This makes it harder for small fish to attack the flies. We then leisurely float around the pond. We can cover this pond easily, so we make a second pass using wet flies—Royal Coachman, Pink Lady, Professor, Yellow Hornberg and Yellow Wooly Worm.

Since the hike is manageable in the dark, we do stay for the evening hatch. These trout are not particularly finicky. Royal Wulff, White Wulff, Bivisible, Pink Lady, Quill Gordon and Elk Hair Caddis. Match size and then color of your fly to the natural. We like to cast to rises and catch trout on their second passes. Action can be nonstop.

The northern hike to East Pond is from Kancamagus Highway. We select this trail because we like to fish Cheney Brook and Pine Brook. These two brooks have often saved the day if we have had a slow outing on East Pond.

We are confident that whichever way you choose to fish East Pond, it will be a memorable day on the water.

The **GREELEY PONDS** are a duo of brook trout goodness a short mile and a half off Kancamagus Highway. These ponds are tiny. Upper Greeley is just over one acre, yet it is twenty-seven feet deep. Lower Greeley, a beaver flowage, is two acres and four feet deep. Both ponds are loaded with brook trout. Upper Greeley does receive fingerlings from Hew Hampshire Fish and Game, though Lower Greeley is all wild brook trout.

Upper Greeley is the pond we spend the most time fishing. You just never know how big of a trout you will catch in this pond. We put the sinking line on our nine-foot, four-weight. We select one of our favorite streamers, including Light Edson Tiger, Ballou Special, Black Ghost, Humungous, Warden's Worry and Harris Special. We get in the pond at the inlet and float right down the middle of the pond. We cast long lines and use the countdown method, casting to the clock. We wait until we find the fish, and then we rejoice.

After we have covered the pond, we get out and go down to Lower Greeley Pond. We put on our floating fly line and fish bushy dry flies, including White Wulff, Grizzly Wulff, PMX Royal, Yellow Stimulator, Pink Bivisible and Elk Hair Caddis. We get into our float tubes on the southwest side of the pond, which is the deepest area, and we just start casting. Small, wild brook trout are aggressive here.

As the sun lowers in the sky, we go back to Upper Greeley Pond to fish the evening hatch. While you could make the effort to match the hatch, we use the flies we were using all afternoon at Lower Greeley Pond. It is a joy to catch trout that are heftier than the fish we were just catching. We usually have had enough fishing before it gets dark, and we head out to the trailhead. We do have our headlamps just in case the fishing was so good we couldn't leave.

Another great duo of ponds is the **SAWYER PONDS**. In fact, we love the entire Sawyer River Watershed. Big Sawyer Pond is large—almost fifty acres and one hundred feet deep. Little Sawyer Pond is only eleven acres but has depths to twenty-eight feet. We love these ponds because of the potential for large brook trout.

Big Sawyer Pond has smelt and chub as forage fish. New Hampshire Fish and Game puts thousands of fingerling brook trout in this pond, and the resident brook trout love them. Needless to say, this is a sinking line, big streamer pond. We bring our nine-foot, six-weight rod. We load the rod with the fastest sinking line we can find. The streamers we use are all size four hooks. If we can't catch a big fish here, then we are not interested. Streamers we like include Gray Ghost, Black Ghost, Ballou Special, Light Edson Tiger, Dark Edson Tiger and Little Brook Trout Bucktail.

Due to the size of Big Sawyer Pond, we look at the prevailing wind to decide where to fish. There is a nice drop-off area at the island. There is another drop-off at the inlet stream for Little Sawyer Pond. There are a couple of deeper holes on the south end of the pond. Use the countdown method and slowly drift around the pond. It takes patience because even fast sink lines can take three or four minutes to reach fish. The action in Big Sawyer Pond will not be fast, but it will be fulfilling.

For fast action, we recommend bushwhacking up the hill to Little Sawyer Pond. Little Sawyer is easy to manage, and the trout are a little more cooperative. We like to fish Little Sawyer with our nine-foot, four-weight outfit. We start with a sink-tip line and our traditional wet flies—Royal Coachman, Professor, Hornberg, Wooly Worm, Silver Prince and Campbell's Fancy. We kick our float tube out thirty feet from shore and cast back to structure. The trout are smaller but more aggressive here. If we have had a hard time on Big Sawyer, Little Sawyer can save the day.

Because the Sawyer Pond trail is easy to navigate, we will fish the evening hatch at Little Sawyer Pond. We fish our favorite dry flies at Little Sawyer Pond, including Elk Hair Caddis, Bivisible, Pink Lady, Royal Wulff, White Wulff and PMX Royal. Match the flies to size of the hatches and then try to match the color. The dry fly fishing on Little Sawyer Pond is fun.

The mile-and-a-half hike into the Sawyer Ponds necessitates that we use float tubes, though we do know guides who carry canoes in to fish these ponds. The hike to the ponds is all uphill, so make a wise choice. Due to the short hike on a well-worn trail, we do not camp overnight, but that is an option. There is a shelter at the pond and ten tent sites.

SAWYER RIVER completes the triumvirate of waters to fish in this watershed. Sawyer River Road climbs along the Sawyer River for three miles until it reaches the Sawyer Pond trailhead. We think nothing of parking at the trailhead and then fishing downstream. Sawyer River is loaded with wild brook trout.

We like to fish with our nine-foot, four-weight outfit. The river is plenty open, and the longer rod lets us cast to pools without dropping a shadow on the water. The trout in this section of the river are super spooky. We are very careful as we approach good-looking stretches of water. We fish wet flies and nymphs in this part of the river. For wet flies, we use Royal Coachman, Professor, Pink Lady, Wooly Worm, Silver Prince and Campbell's Fancy. For nymphs, we like Hare's Ear, Pheasant Tail, Copper John, Casual Dress, Halfback and Rainbow Warrior.

If we choose to fish our way back to the parking area, we will fish bushy dry flies—Royal Wulff, White Wulff, Grizzly Wulff and PMX Royal—in the long riffle runs and deep pools. These flies will bring a response from the aggressive wild trout. If we lose track of time and end up far downstream, we climb out of the valley and up to the road and walk back to our vehicle. The Sawyer River has never disappointed us.

When we are more into a wilderness fishing adventure, we take the Sawyer River trail upstream. We hike to the Hancock Notch trail and walk until we see the river. We then drop down into the river and fish. This is some spectacular wild brook trout fishing, and we never see another boot print on the riverbed. The trout are smaller, but they are plentiful. The action is nonstop. When we know we are only going to fish this piece of river, we bring our seven-foot, three-weight outfit. We use the same flies as the lower river. We fish barbless flies. These trout should all be released with as little hook damage as possible. The trout are that precious.

ZEALAND VALLEY is a unique brook trout fishing experience. Starting at Zealand Road off Route 302 in Carroll, we will drive in as far as we can. Sometimes parking limitations will dictate where we can park. We avail ourselves to the AMC shuttle service when it is available. When we get to the farthest trailhead, it is a quick two-mile hike to Zealand Falls and the Zealand Falls hut.

The Zealand Falls are pretty, and they are the start of the brook trout fishing. A pond and a couple of beaver flowages hold wild brook trout. We will go off trail to get to these pieces of water, but it is worth the effort. These trout have a unique look to them, and you will tell immediately as you fish downstream and start to catch hatchery trout.

We like to fish the Zealand River with our seven-foot, three-weight outfit. We use a floating fly line, with wet flies in the river and dry flies on the flowages. Wet flies we like include Professor, Hare's Ear, Pink Lady, Sparkle Emerger, Silver Prince and Campbell's Fancy. We fish these in any riffle water or long pools that run in the river. When we find any beaver flowages or sections of flatwater, we switch to bushy dry flies, such as White Wulff, Yellow Humpy, Bivisible, Elk Hair Caddis, Stimulator and PMX Royal. We fish these flies in sizes fourteen or sixteen. The brook trout will literally jump right out of the water and attack these flies.

It will take most of the day to fish the over two miles of stream to the parking lot. We take our time and stop at a quiet pool to have lunch. Soak in the beauty of your surroundings. This is one of our most relaxing expeditions, as we always catch trout, and it is always beautiful.

When we choose to fish for the mix of hatchery fish and wild fish, we will walk the road and look for any places where feeder streams enter the Zealand River. Trout congregate in these locations in the summer when water temperatures rise. We only use barbless hooks when we decide to do this type of fishing because we want to keep the stress on these fish at a minimum. Once we start to catch hatchery fish exclusively, we call it a day and go find a pond to fish the evening hatch.

KANACAMAGUS HIGHWAY, a two-lane road, bisects the White Mountain National Forest and crosses many streams. When we want to go on a hit-and-run brook trout expedition, we head to the "Kanc." Whether we decide to start in the east at Conway or the west at Lincoln, we get to see the entire scope of the White Mountain National Forest. This is wild brook trout fishing.

Climbing out of Lincoln, one of the first places we hit is the Hancock Branch of the **Pemigewasset River**. We park at the Hancock recreation area and get as far away from the campground as we can, and then we start to fish. This is a great place to get started with the stream brook trout of the Kanc. There's not a lot of area to cover—just a quick-hitting section of stream to get the juices flowing.

The next area we stop at is the Otter Rocks picnic area. We hike to fish the junction pool of the Hancock and Pine Brooks. We are never disappointed. Even at the height of the summer, we catch brook trout in this area.

Continuing east, our next stop is the Sawyer River trailhead. We don't hike very far along this trail. You go downhill and arrive at the **Swift River** within minutes. The Swift River is just a brook here. There are large slabs of granite that create nice plunge pools and long runs. Due to the color of the granite, the wild brook trout are almost a silver color, making the blue spot halos even brighter than normal—just gorgeous fish. We enjoy this section of river so much that we often lose track of time. If we happen to be ahead of schedule, we will ford the Swift River and make a quick run up to the beaver flowages on Meadow Brook. Just don't lose track of time.

Headwaters of the Swift River.

Fall is a prime time for brook trout.

Our next stop is at **Sabbaday Falls**, which is a short hike from the parking area. The fishing begins above Sabbaday Falls. We like to hike to where an unnamed tributary joins Sabbaday Brook. This is about a mile past the falls. The trout in Sabbaday are not very big, but there are a lot of them. It is another quick stop before we venture on.

Oliverian Brook is not a quick hitter. It really deserves a whole morning or afternoon to appreciate the water and its wild brook trout. We take the Oliverian Brook trail to the junction with the Passaconway Cut Off trail. We then bushwhack down to the brook. Since Hurricane Irene, Oliverian Brook has become the poster child for woody debris in a stream. The fishing will be challenging but very rewarding.

Champney Brook is the next stop on our Kanc wild brook trout tour. Park at the trailhead for Champney Falls trail. The hike to the falls is approximately a mile and a half. This is the opposite of Sabbaday Falls. Here we fish from the base of the falls back to the parking lot. The brook above Champney Falls can get pretty small in the summer, so we try to avoid fishing there. Downstream from the falls is classic White Mountain water—riffle runs and plunge pools that all have small wild brook trout.

The final stop on our Kanc tour is the **Lower Falls**. This is one of the deepest spots on the Swift River, and it holds big trout. These trout are very finicky. They get jumped on and swam over all day by the recreational water users. We have found that if we wait until dark and put on a big heavy fly, we can tempt one of these monsters with Woolly Bugger, Casual Dress, Humungous or Complex Twist Bugger—all with either a beadhead or a conehead to get to the bottom of the pool.

Bear Notch Road holds two great wild brook trout streams. When we are traveling on Bear Notch Road, we try to fish these streams. Cutting through the experimental forest, we find that the stream corridors are some of the oldest trees in the White Mountain National Forest, which makes for excellent wilderness fishing.

Heading north off the Kanc, the first stream we see after crossing the Swift River is Douglas Brook. We park at the Rob Brook Road bike trailhead and walk to Douglas Brook. We immediately feel the coolness of the pines that form the riparian area of the brook. This is prime wild brook trout water. We fish upstream quickly, but our focus is on heading downstream. There is great riffle water and woody debris that make for prime brook trout holding water. Fish every piece of water, but if there is not a strike quickly, move on to the next piece of water.

We like to use our seven-foot, three-weight outfit here. Douglas Brook is classic wet fly fishing. We use Royal Coachman, Orange Fish Hawk, Professor, Silver Prince, Campbell's Fancy and Silver Doctor. Brook trout have been taking these flies for decades, and we have seen no let up here.

The trout are that nice deep black color and have a look all their own. We have been fishing Douglas Brook for fifty years, and the fishing is as amazing now as it has always been. We know that you will enjoy your day on this water.

Farther north on Bear Notch Road is a series of Forest Service roads that go deep into the heart of the Bartlett Experimental Forest. Fire Road 44 is bikeable and hikeable. This road takes us to Louisville Brook. Louisville Brook is lightly fished and has some of the bigger brook trout that we find in the White Mountain National Forest. Since FR 44 crosses the brook in several places, it is easy to fish Louisville Brook in sections.

The first section is up the Attitash trail. We will do this early in the season when the brook has fishable water. The little brook trout here are beautiful. We catch a bunch of them and release all of them. Then we hit the fire roads and head downstream. The water is classic White Mountain brook trout water—riffle runs, plunge pools and woody debris. There are wild brook trout everywhere. We are always surprised when a fat, foot-long brook trout slams our fly. It is something that gets ingrained into our memory banks. It will be ingrained in your memory banks as well.

PROVINCE POND is a quiet, little pond on the New Hampshire–Maine border. Province Pond is a mile-and-a-half hike from the parking lot off Route 113. Province Pond is twelve acres and has some depth at eleven feet. There is a Forest Service shelter on Province Pond, making it ideal for an overnight expedition. We always hike in with our float tubes to fish Province Pond

We start with our nine-foot, four-weight outfit and a sink-tip line at Province Pond, using small streamers like Harris Special, Mickey Finn, Light Edson Tiger, Dark Edson Tiger, Warden's Worry and Black Ghost. We use the countdown method in the deep areas and fish the structure along the shoreline.

If we don't get action with streamers, we switch to wet flies, including Quill Gordon, Light Cahill, Hornberg, Wooly Worm, Royal Coachman and Professor. We fish these flies just under the surface, and it is fun to see trout rocket up off the bottom of the pond and attack the fly.

At dusk or dawn, we like to fish dry flies at Province Pond. We use White Wulff, PMX Royal, Lime Humpy, Devil Bug, Pink Bivisible and Elk Hair Caddis. In the morning, we use these flies in size ten to try to draw strikes from the fish that have been feeding all night. In the evening, we try to match the size of the bugs and then the color. We love the dry fly fishing on this pond.

3.

UPPER VALLEY REGION

Trout Pond in Lyme is one of the secret gems that is right under everyone's nose. It is located a short hike off Trout Pond Lane, and we have never seen another angler here. Lyme is just north of Hanover, home of Dartmouth College and the Dartmouth Hitchcock Medical Center. We are pleased that Trout Pond has not been found by the masses.

Trout Pond is only twelve acres, making it the perfect float tube pond. It has an average depth of eighteen feet and a hole just off the north shore that measures well over forty feet deep. Needless to say, we start fishing Trout Pond with our sinking fly line. This pond is made for using the countdown method and fishing the clock. We start with our streamers, as there is the potential to catch some large brook trout. Harris Special, Warden's Worry, Mickey Finn, Fish Skull Bugger, Hornberg and Humungous are our favorites. As Trout Pond is stocked by helicopter by New Hampshire Fish and Game, we carry the Little Brook Trout Bucktail in our box if we are fishing at that time.

If we take the trail to the western shore, we float right across the pond, west to east. This takes us right across the different depths of Trout Pond, helping us locate trout. As we approach the eastern shore, we spend more time here. This is where the pond drops to more than forty feet deep and allows us to find the level where fish are located.

Because we can get in and out of this pond in a reasonable time, we do fish the evening hatch. Dry flies and emergers used in combination can be highly effective. If we are using a dry/dropper rig, we will select a high floating dry fly like the Royal Wulff or PMX Royal and tie an emerger off

A fine pond dweller.

the back. Emergers that we use at Trout Pond include Poly-Wing Emerger, Winged Biot Emerger, Sparkle Soft Hackle, Bi Focal Emerger and Orange Fish Hawk. We start fishing this way at dusk or at the first sign of a hatch. Most time the brook trout will take the emerger. When they start to take or hit the dry, we switch to dry flies only.

Dry flies we like at Trout Pond include Pink Lady Bivisible, Dun Variant, Brown Klinkhammer, Olive Klinkhammer, Light Cahill and Purple Parachute Adams. Match the size of the hatch and then try to get close to the color. We find that size matters most when dry fly fishing Trout Pond. We fish the shallower portions of Trout Pond during the hatch, focusing on the inlet at the east end of the pond or the outlet at the northwest end of the pond.

MINK BROOK is a stream that runs right through the town of Hanover. It is the main stem of a watershed that holds a good amount of wild brook trout. The majority of the watershed is protected by land purchases and conservation easements by the Hanover Conservancy—great foresight by that organization. There are over twenty-six miles of wild brook trout habitat in this watershed.

There are designated paths along the lower stretches of Mink Brook, which makes access easy for fishing. We don't think that many people fish Mink Brook, as we always get strange looks when we go there. This is a seven-foot, three-weight brook if there ever was one. The brook has many great plunge pools and lots of woody debris—all great locations to find a wild brook trout. We fish wet flies here, as room to cast a dry fly is minimal. Wet flies we like are Sparkle Soft Hackle, Brown Hackle, Gray Hackle, Wooly Worm, Royal Coachman and Silver Prince.

New Hampshire Fish and Game does stock a minimal amount of hatchery trout in this brook. We have never caught a "stockie" in Mink Brook. Most likely, the namesake mink make quick work of any hatchery trout.

Many roads cross over the brooks in the Mink Brook Watershed. Hop into these brooks with your fly rod and catch wild brook trout. You will be amazed that you are catching these jewels within the hustle and bustle of the Dartmouth College area.

ROCKY POND in Wentworth is a different kind of pond for us. There is a lot of rocky structure in the pond, which makes great cover for the trout and good homes for the insect life. Rocky Pond is a good drive off woods roads, but the final hike-in is manageable. We have bushwhacked a canoe into Rocky Pond, but the best part of the pond is easily accessed by float tube. Why not take the easy way in? Rocky Pond is twenty acres with an average depth of eight feet. There is a nice hole, over twenty feet deep, on the southern section of the pond.

Rocky Pond is a three-line pond. We start with our sink-tip line and traditional wet flies—Royal Coachman, Professor, Pink Lady, Silver Prince, Campbell's Fancy and Hare's Ear. We kick our float tubes about thirty feet from shore and then cast back to the structure. We use the countdown method to determine the correct depth for the flies. We work our way down the western shore until we hit the big bump out in the southern end of the pond.

We quickly switch to our sinking line. We put on a short, six-foot leader and select a streamer from Light Edson Tiger, Ballou Special, Black Ghost, Rubber Bugger or Franke Shiner. We then start to float our way north to the opposite shore. This can be tough to accomplish on a windy day. We again use the countdown method. Early in the season, brook trout will be close to the surface. In the summer, we need all twenty-four feet before we can locate fish.

As evening approaches, we switch to our floating line and dry flies. We float our tubes into the outlet cove and get ready for action, using Quill Gordon, Light Cahill, Adams, Balloon Caddis, Klinkhammer and Griffith Gnat. Match the size of the hatch that is coming off and then the color. We have only caught smaller brook trout on dry flies in the cove, but the action was nonstop. Now you know our secret.

DERBY POND is one of only a few brook trout ponds in New Hampshire that is not stocked, at least not on a regular basis. We like this pond because we feel like we are catching brook trout that were deposited here after the last glacier receded. The fish are beautiful, and we think that they have an appearance all their own. Mother Nature is the only one who knows for sure.

Since we treat Derby Pond as a wild brook trout pond, we break out all our traditional flies. Wet flies include Royal Coachman, Silver Prince, Campbell's Fancy, Silver Doctor, Montreal and Professor. Dry flies include Bivisible, Hendrickson, Light Cahill, Renegade, Adams and Pink Lady. Fishing for the small wild brook trout is nonstop if we arrive at the pond and the trout are on the feed.

Derby Pond is only six acres, making it ideal for the float tube. There is some depth to the pond at twelve feet. We fish our wet flies with a sink-tip line and our dry flies with a floating line. This pond doesn't hold any large brook trout, so just go there to enjoy a fun afternoon or evening of wild brook trout fishing.

Derby Pond is accessed off the Bryant Pond Road in Dorchester. There is a trail on the left, about a mile after you have passed Bryant Pond.

COLE POND is a quality fishing pond, as designated by New Hampshire Fish and Game. This is another pond that is close to the Hanover area and is a jewel so near to that population center. The hike into Cole Pond is all uphill. It is a seventeen-acre pond with an average depth of twenty-six feet and a hole that is fifty-nine feet deep. Cole Pond can be found in the Enfield Wildlife Management Area in Enfield. The trail to Cole Pond is off Bog Road.

When you reach the pond, bear left and take the trail to the abandoned fireplace. We guess that at one point this was a homestead on Cole Pond. You can easily launch your float tube here, as there is a rock ledge that slopes right into the pond. This is also a place where the pond slopes drastically right down to the deepest part.

We use our nine-foot, five-weight rod outfits equipped with full sink lines. This is a deep and slow fishing pond that requires the use of the countdown method and fishing the clock. The big trout in Cole Pond tend to prefer baitfish or brook trout fingerlings. The fingerlings are courtesy of the New Hampshire Fish and Game aerial stocking program. The Little Brook Trout Bucktail is your friend after this stocking. Other streamers we select are Soft Hackle Streamer, Light Edson Tiger, Supervisor, Franke Shiner, Warden's Worry and Harris Special.

The larger trout are hard to locate in this pond. We look for schools of bait fish breaking the surface and trying to escape the predatory large brook trout. We then focus on that section of the pond, trying different streamers. The fishing here is neither fast nor furious. It can be frustrating, but it can be very rewarding.

Butterfield Pond is located on the edge of the Gile State Forest in Wilmot. There is trail access to the pond. We like Butterfield Pond because of the twelve-acre size, which is ideal for the float tube. Butterfield Pond also has depth. There is a large hole that is over twenty feet deep located on the southern end of the pond. The second hole is a small spring-fed depression on the eastern part of the pond.

When we arrive at Butterfield Pond, we have our nine-foot, four-weight with a sink-tip line. We start with our favorite wet flies, using the countdown method and Yellow Wooly Worm, Yellow Hornberg, Professor, Campbell's Fancy and Yellow Sparkle Emerger. We float along the shoreline between thirty and forty feet out in the pond, casting back toward shore. When we reach the southern end of Butterfield Pond, we slowly float north. This takes us right over the deepest part of the pond. Take more time to let your wet fly sink here. Fish may be at lower depths, depending on the time of year.

When we reach shallower water, we will switch to a streamer and kick back over the deep water. Streamers to use include the Gray Ghost, Black Ghost, Maynard Marvel and Harris Special. If you are at Butterfield Pond in June, try the Little Brook Trout Bucktail. Butterfield Pond receives brook trout fingerlings from New Hampshire Fish and Game.

Evenings on Butterfield Pond can be a dry fly angler's delight. When the hatches are on, the brook trout get aggressive. We like to sit in our float tube, wait for a rise and then cast right next to the rise. Most of the time, we catch fish that think they missed the original or are just being efficient and grabbing another bug. We only cast to rises. Casting any other time disturbs the water surface and will scare the fish outside of comfortable casting range. Be Patient.

We like to use classic dry flies on Butterfield Pond, including Adams, Quill Gordon, Hendrickson, Light Cahill, Elk Hair Caddis and Griffth's Gnat. Match your fly to the size of the hatch and then try to match the color.

Oh, the second hole on the east shore—that is for you to find. We have to keep some things a secret.

LAKE SOLITUDE in Newbury is a jewel tucked away in the Sunapee Mountain Range. It is not easy to access. The trail that we choose to access the pond is challenging. We like to use the Andrew Brook trail, and it has several brook crossings. The trail gets very steep as we approach the pond. We have never seen another angler while fishing Lake Solitude.

Lake Solitude is small—only six acres. It is perfect for the float tube. Lake Solitude does have a spot that is more than twenty feet deep. This is our area of focus. We use our nine-foot, four-weight rod with a sink-tip line in Lake Solitude. We use the countdown method to locate the brook trout. We use a combination of wet flies and streamers. For wet flies, we use Royal Coachman, Brown Hackle, Gray Hackle, Wooly Worm, Pink Lady and White Miller. For streamers, we like Harris Special, Maynard Marvel, Rubber Bugger and Complex Twist Bugger. All streamers should be size ten or smaller. Lake Solitude receives fingerling brook trout from New Hampshire Fish and Game. Have some Little Brook Trout Bucktails in your fly box.

The edges of Lake Solitude have quite a few aquatic plants as the season progresses. If we visit the lake in the summer, we float along the edges of the plants and cast toward the deeper water. We use the countdown method and fan cast from the edges of the plants, out into the deeper water and back to the plants. We often let our sink-tip line drag the floating line down into the water—whatever it takes to locate the trout.

Because of the distance and difficulty of the hike to Lake Solitude, we have not fished the evening hatch. We are confident that the dry fly action here will be like any other remote pond. We just do not feel safe trying to traverse down the mountain with float tube and headlamp in the dark. For this reason, we leave Lake Solitude about two hours before sunset, and we fish Andrew Brook. Andrew Brook is a fun, little native brook trout water. Plunge pools and large woody debris leave lots of brook trout cover for this mountain stream. We use the same wet flies in Andrew Brook that we use in Lake Solitude. It is a fine way to end a day of brook trout fishing.

4.

MONADNOCK REGION

We want to briefly touch on the wild brook trout fishing in the Mount Monadnock region and the southwest corner of New Hampshire. Any stream that has a cold water source in this region of New Hampshire holds wild brook trout. Meadow Brook in Sharon, Sand Brook in Hillsboro, Gulf Brook in Chesterfield are great examples. Find brooks that mimic these, and you will find native brook trout. The Monadnock region is closest to the big population centers of New Hampshire. We feel the need to keep these waters secret until such time that New Hampshire Fish and Game gives these streams the same protections that they have afforded to the streams we named.

If you live in this region, or visit frequently, pack a fly rod with you. If you have a moment, get out and explore. You may find your own secret waters.

EPILOGUE

The breakfast dishes were all cleaned and put away. The beds were stripped, and Troutman would take them home to wash and fold. The Boys had loaded their vehicles and were ready to return to the real world.

"What a great trip," said Pic.

"Not sure how each year gets better," said Goose.

"Because we enjoy each other's company as much as we enjoy the fishing," said Troutman.

The Old Timer nodded in agreement.

"Where we going next year?" asked Troutman.

"We should just come back here," said Pic.

"Let's go fish the Magalloway area," said Goose. "I'd like a shot at those big brook trout.

"We have plenty of time," said the Old Timer. "Savor this trip for a while."

Everyone shook hands and headed back to civilization. Visions of beautiful wild brook trout danced in their heads.

Over the winter, the Old Timer passed to the big brook trout waters. Troutman's college buddy from the University of New Hampshire LC joined the group. He was eager to learn the craft of fly fishing and head into the wilderness—something he didn't have in California.

LC learned quickly, and it was a renewal for Troutman to teach his friend to fly fish and to appreciate wild brook trout. As he had done with Pic and Goose, Troutman passed down everything he had learned from the Old Timer. The Old Timer would be proud that someone so worthy had taken his place.

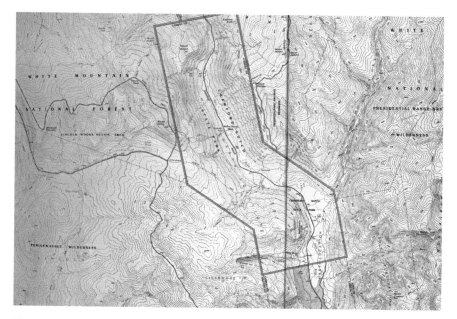

Crawford Notch holds many secret waters.

The Boys continue to explore the secret waters of New Hampshire. Each year Troutman ties the flies—some new patterns and some traditional patterns. The Boys continue to enjoy one another's company and to catch wild brook trout in wilderness places. We hope that you will too.

Fishing in the wild places of New Hampshire requires preplanning and knowledge to have a fun and safe trip. Whenever float tubing, we wear the inflatable suspenders. When hiking, we purchase a Hike Safe card from New Hampshire Fish and Game. This covers us if we need to be evacuated by New Hampshire Fish and Game. We leave a detailed explanation of where we are going on the table at camp. This is wilderness fishing. While the trails are often well defined, we never know when an injury will occur on the trail. It is always better to be safe than sorry.

We have tried to supply you with the most up-to-date information for finding New Hampshire's secret waters. Woods roads, hiking trails and right of ways have a way of changing yearly. Please check the most up-to-date information from the sources listed in the bibliography before attempting to reach any waters that are wilderness or remote.

Appendix

HARD TO FIND FLIES

Many of the flies that we use on the Secret Waters can be found at well-stocked fly shops like North Country Angler in North Conway or Tall Timber Fly Shop in Pittsburg. When tying your own flies, the internet has many of the formulas, and many sites even have video lessons. Hit the search engines and tie to your heart's content.

We like to use some of the old-time patterns or patterns we have adapted. The following patterns are those that are not easily found on an internet search but are highly effective for Secret Waters brook trout.

Alder Fly
Hook: Size 12 dry fly
Thread: Olive
Body: UV peacock dubbing
Wing: Dark fine dark deer hair
Head: Butt ends of deer hair
Antenna: Dun micro fibetts

Devil Bug (Doodle Bug)
Hook: Size 8–14 dry fly 2x
Thread: Hot orange or hot green
Body: Red or peacock
Tail, top and head: Contrasting
    deer or elk hair

Little Marryat
Hook: Size 14 dry fly
Thread: Gray
Tail: Gray brown rusty dun
Body: Light gray fur
Wing: Starling
Hackle: Gray brown rusty dun

Pink Lady Bivisible
Hook: Size 12–14 dry fly
Thread: Hot pink
Tail: Light ginger hackle
Body: Pink floss
Wing: none
Hackle: Light ginger tied palmer
Shoulder hackle: Chartreuse

Quill Gordon
Hook: Size 12–16 dry fly
Thread: Brown
Tail: Rusty blue dun
Body: Peacock quill ribbed with fine gold wire
Wing: Lemon wood duck tied wing back over body
Hackle: Medium Blue Dun

Variants
Hook: Size 12–14 dry fly
Thread: Chartreuse
Tail: Hackle fibers to match body hackle
Body: Choose gold, silver, quill
Wing: Your favorite slate gray quill
Hackle: One hackle to match hook size and one hackle larger (we like dun)

Fullback Nymph
Hook: Size 8–12, 2x long nymph
Thread: Black
Tail: Pheasant tail barbs
Abdomen: Peacock herl
Rib: Black thread
Thorax: Bushy peacock herl
Cover: Pheasant tail fibers full length of fly
Legs: Barbs of pheasant tail

Pink Lady Nymph
Hook: Size 12, 2x wet fly
Thread: Orange
Tail: Cream hackle fibers
Abdomen: Light yellow floss twisted to create segments
Thorax: Light beige dubbing
Crown: Gray silk floss
Legs: Strips of starling wing

"88"
Hook: Size 10–14 wet fly
Thread: Hot red
Tail: None
Body: Rear two thirds hot red yarn, front third olive floss
Wing: Lemon wood duck
Hackle: One grizzly on wet, two grizzly on dry

Brown Hackle
Hook: Size 12–16 wet fly
Thread: Black
Tail: Red wool trimmed at hook bend
Body: Peacock herl
Hackle: Brown grizzly palmered
Wing: None

Campbell's Fancy
Hook: Size 8–14 wet fly
Thread: Black
Tail: Golden pheasant crest or yellow hackle fibers
Body: Gold tinsel
Hackle: Brown tied palmer two turns at head
Wing: Teal

Gray Hackle
Hook Size 12–16 wet fly
Thread: Gray
Tail: Red wool trimmed at hook bend
Body: Peacock herl
Hackle: Badger palmered
Wing: None

Leisenrings Tup's

Hook: Size 12–14 wet fly
Thread: Yellow
Tail: Light blue dun
Body: Back-yellow twist front-claret
    dubbing on yellow thread
Collar: Light blue dun

Silver Doctor

Hook: Size 6–14 wet fly
Thread: Red
Tail: Golden pheasant tippets
Body: Flat silver tinsel
Throat: Silver doctor blue hackle
    fibers
Wing: Married turkey, blue goose,
    red goose, yellow goose

Silver Prince

Hook: Size 10–14 wet fly
Thread: Black
Tail: Three peacock herl
Body: Silver tinsel wrapped halfway
    down bend
Ribbing: Oval tinsel
Wing: Lemon wood duck
Hackle: Black hackle

Yellow Wooly Worm

Hook: Size 10–14 wet fly
Thread: Yellow
Tail: Red wool trimmed at hook
    bend
Body: Yellow chenille
Hackle: Grizzly tied palmer

Harris Special

Hook: Size 6–14 streamer
Thread: Black
Tail: Golden pheasant tippets
Body: Flat silver tinsel
Throat: Red bucktail sparse and
    long
Wing: Sparse white bucktail veiled
    with lemon wood duck (mallard
    dyed wood duck is less effective)

Maynard's Marvel

Hook: Size 8–14, 4xl streamer
Thread: Black or red
Tail: Red hackle fibers
Body: Embossed silver tinsel
Throat: Red hackle fibers
Wing: Mallard over light blue calf
    tail over golden pheasant crest

BIBLIOGRAPHY

New Hampshire Atlas and Gazetteer. 14ᵗʰ ed. Yarmouth, ME: Delorme Publishing, 2002.

New Hampshire Fish and Game Department. "Depth Maps of Select NH Lakes and Ponds." https://www.wildlife.state.nh.us.

———. "Freshwater Stocking Summary by Waterbody." https://www.wildlife.state.nh.us.

Rolfe, Edward M. *Exploring New Hampshire's White Mountains*. Twin Mountain, NH: Wilderness Map Company, 2017.

Smith, Steven D. *White Mountain Guide: AMC's Comprehensive Guide to Hiking Trails in the White Mountain National Forest*. 30ᵗʰ ed. Boston, MA: Appalachian Mountain Club, 2017.

Stewart, Dick, and Farrow Allen. *Flies for Trout*. North Conway, NH: Mountain Pond, 1993.

Sturgis, William Bayard. *Fly-Tying*. New York: Charles Scribner and Sons, 1940.

Surette, Dick. *Trout and Salmon Fly Index*. Harrisburg, PA: Stackpole Books, 1968.

ABOUT THE AUTHOR

Steve Angers, a native of New Hampshire, has spent more than fifty years in the pursuit of and preservation of wild brook trout. Since catching his first brook trout at the base of Champney Falls in 1964, he has traveled far and wide through New England's beautiful landscapes, ultimately returning to New Hampshire. Steve is an accomplished fly tyer who enjoys old-school patterns as well as creating new patterns. When Steve isn't fishing, he works with Trout Unlimited protecting wild brook trout habitat. Steve owns and operates the North Country Angler in North Conway.